C000226459

Free Lace

Patterns

Free Lace Patterns

Sheila Brown

B. T. Batsford Ltd, London

First published 1990

ISBN 0 7134 6504 2

Typeset by Deltatype, Ellesmere Port

And printed by
The Bath Press, Bath

For the publishers
B. T. Batsford Limited
4 Fitzhardinge Street
London W1H 0AH

Contents

Acknowledgement	7
Introduction	9
Hints on technique	11
Torchon edging	12
Torchon insertion	14
Furnishing edging	16
Spring (snowdrops)	21
Summer (strawberries)	23
Autumn (barley ears)	26
Winter (holly leaves)	28
Galaxy	30
Spider's web	32
Animal motifs	35
Edging 1	45
Edging 2	47
Edging 3	49
Rose	51
Bowl of tulips	53
Bridge coasters	56
Corner motif 1	58
Corner motif 2	60
Motif 3	62
Decoration	64
Table mat 1	67
Poppy	70
Sunburst	74
Oval mat	77
Fan	79
Table mat 2	84
Suppliers and sources of information	87

Acknowledgement

Many people have helped in the making of this book, by means of inspiration, advice and encouragement.

My special thanks go to Tordis Berendt, who guided my first steps in lace and has, over the years since, followed and supported my efforts. Good friends Beryl Ellington and Kathleen Cameron have combed the manuscript, discussed the ideas, and checked the instructions. Noel H. G. Choat, of Wethersfield, Essex, kindly allowed me to adapt patterns from his grandmother's collection, and brought to light a late French influence in East Anglian lacemaking. My grateful thanks are also due to Bridget Cook, Geraldine Stott and Edna Sutton for permission to use their books as references to help the newer lacemaker.

Added to these must be the ladies of Sawbridgeworth Lacemakers and of the Harlow Adult Education classes, who have over many years kept my nose to the grindstone and made lacemaking for me a source of great enjoyment. Needless to say, any errors are mine alone.

Introduction

Every piece of lace is distinctive. No matter how simple the design, two lacemakers will produce two different products.

Each lacemaker, no matter how fresh or experienced, makes lace to express her or his personality. It is the *creative* urge which produces lace – not the repetitive or mundane.

This book aims to help each lacemaker extend her own creative horizon, and to impose her own ideas on the work in front of her. This may mean changing stitches, techniques or threads – to say nothing of the modern (but so old!) use of colour. In this way, a basic design can become fresh and original.

A faithful copy of a beautiful design is a joy forever, but today's multitude of lacemakers wish increasingly to put more of themselves into their work, and these pages are intended to help them do just that.

Stitches, fillings and footsides can be changed to give different interpretations. *Autumn* (page 26), if worked using ten stick, takes on one form; worked in half-stitch plaits it assumes quite another. And so with many, many other patterns.

Genius is not required. Inventiveness and the joy of simple creation are the only necessary ingredients after a knowledge of the basic stitches and techniques.

Sheila Brown
1990

Hints on technique

1. If working in 'free standing' half stitch, always do a cloth stitch and twist for strength before and after the pin.
2. Where pairs have to be added, as in the handkerchief motifs (pages 58–61), or for fillings, a neat method is to wind one bobbin, take the thread through the pinhole – from which the pin has been removed – replace the pin and wind the thread back on to a second bobbin. Thus the addition of four or more threads may be done smoothly.
3. ● on the patterns means 'start here'.
4. The threads used may be changed for others of similar thicknesses, if preferred.
5. i) For mounting on to felt or other fabrics, leave long ends which can then be taken through the fabric and tied off.

   ii) For unmounted work, bow off and where possible weave ends into the lace for neatness, or tie off and cut the ends.

Abbreviations

The following abbreviations are used for books mentioned in the text:

BBLS Bridget Cook and Geraldine Stott, *The Book of Bobbin Lace Stitches*, Batsford

BFL Edna Sutton, *Bruges Flower Lace*, Dryad Press

PS Bridget Cook, *Practical Skills in Bobbin Lace*, Batsford

Torchon edging

Brok 100/2

Method of working

1. Using eighteen pairs, start as in *PS*, Section I.6 or I.8.
2. The diamonds are worked in Torchon ground, Dieppe ground or spiders; tallies could also be used.
3. When working the corner, put two twists on the pairs left off to give a neater appearance.
4. i) Right-hand footside. Work as in *PS*, Section I,37.

   ii) Left-hand footside. Work cloth stitch and twist, pin, cloth stitch and twist.

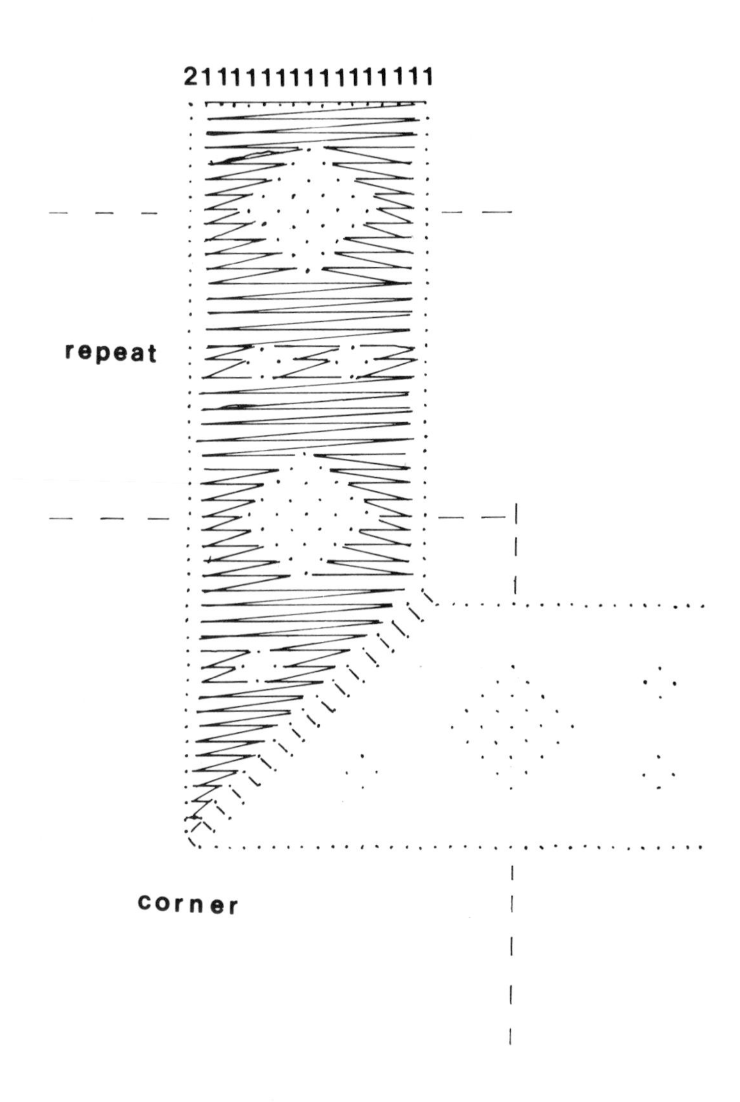

Torchon insertion

Brok 80
or Madiera Supertwist 30

This may be worked as a fine insertion, using Heading 1, or as a streamer for a wedding bouquet using Heading 2. If the pattern is enlarged to have 8 mm between the vertical pins instead of 4 mm, then a three-ply knitting thread may be used to make strips that can be assembled into slipover tops, stoles, etc. In this case, instead of working spiders, the pairs work through each other in cloth stitch (see below).

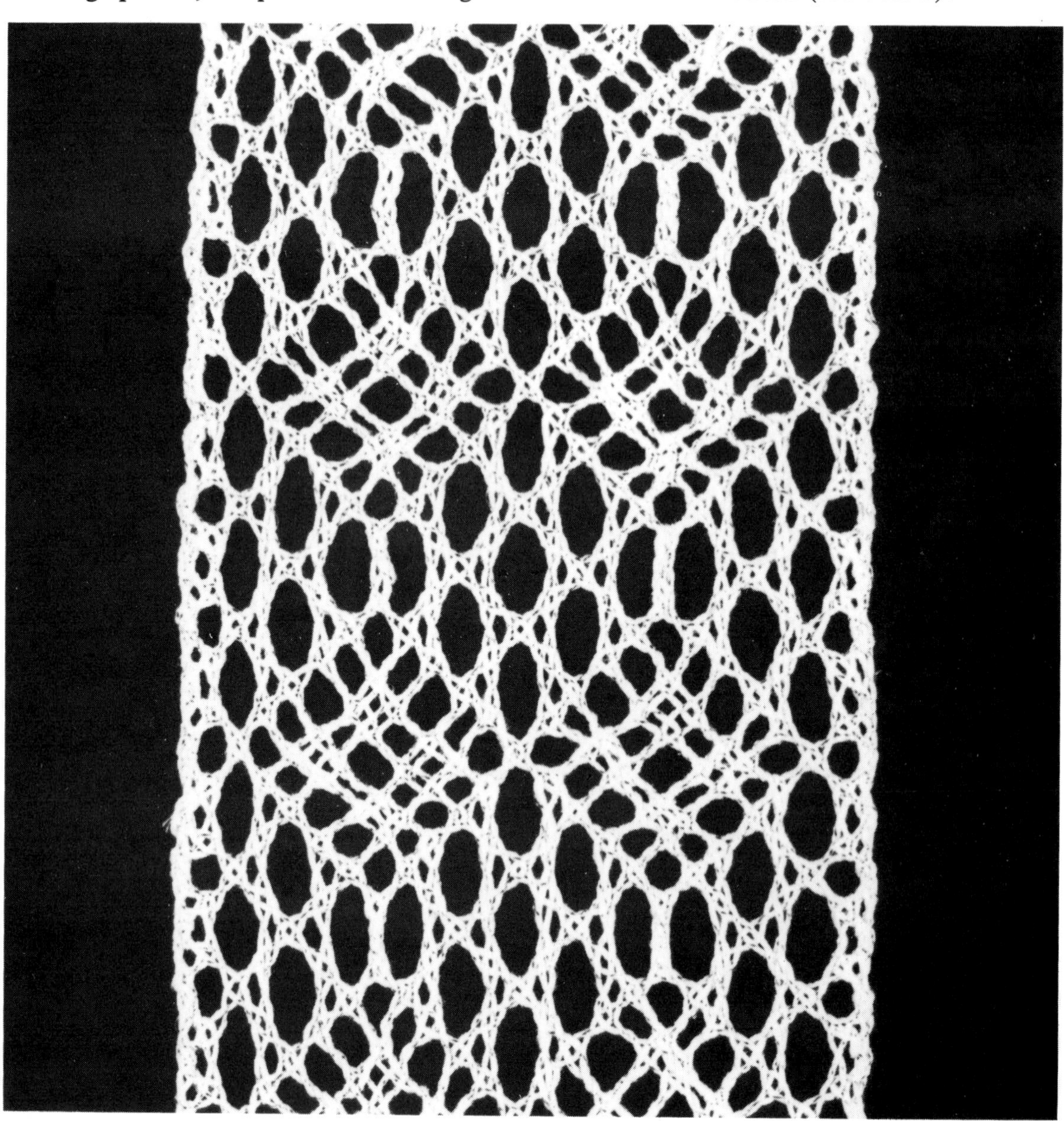

Method of working

Depending on the type of footside used, you will require 26 or 28 pairs.

1. For heading 1: work as in *PS*, Section I,7 to start and reverse these directions to finish off.

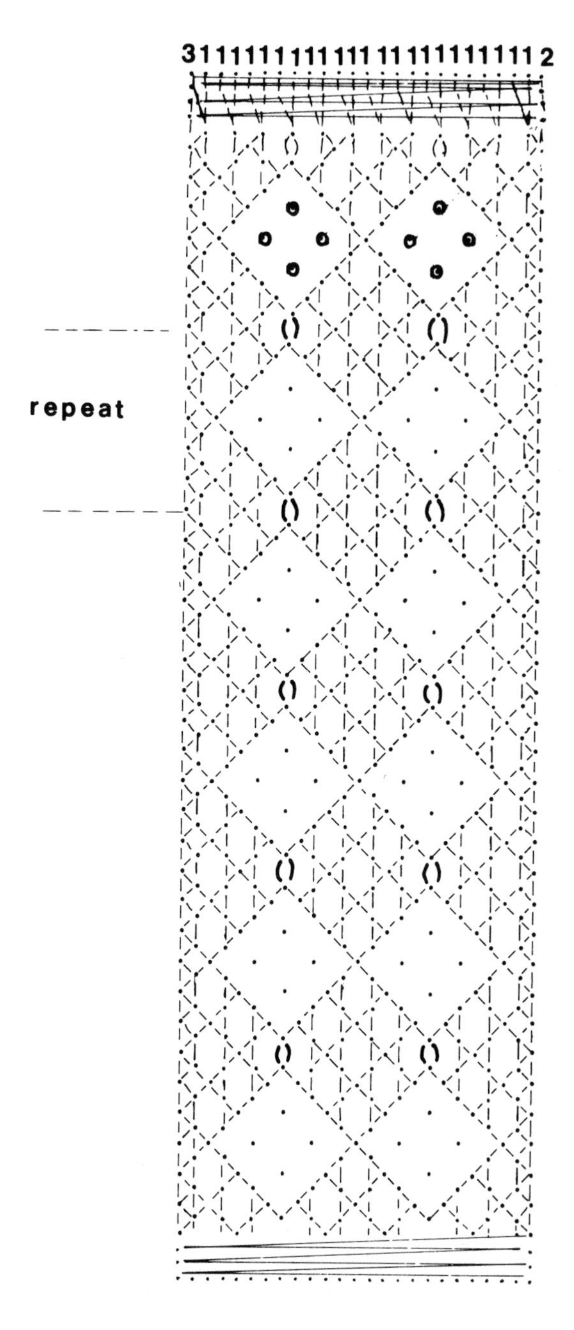

2. For heading 2: hang two pairs open on '**A**', other pairs on support pins and work as follows: (a) cover pin '**A**' with cloth stitch and twist (b) work half stitch, pin, half stitch to bring in the other pairs (c) footside as in Edging 1, page 45.

3. ( ) denotes a pinbar, i.e. work a half stitch, put up the pin and cover with a half stitch. Put a pin into the next lower vertical pinhole and cover with a half stitch. An extra twist may be put on the intermediate half stitch.

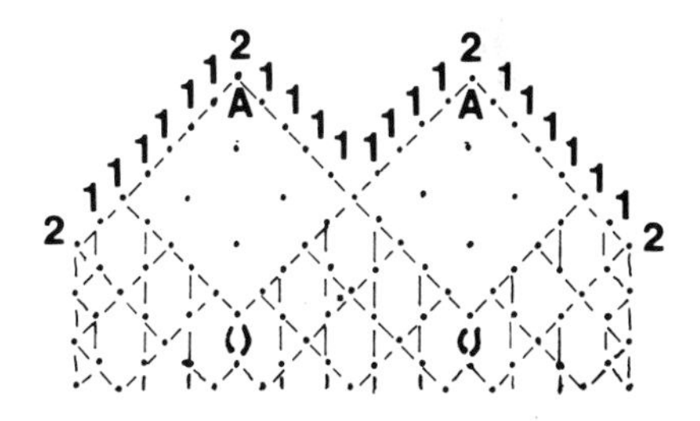

Furnishing edging

Bockens 50/2

This can be used as an edging for curtains, blinds, table cloths, etc.

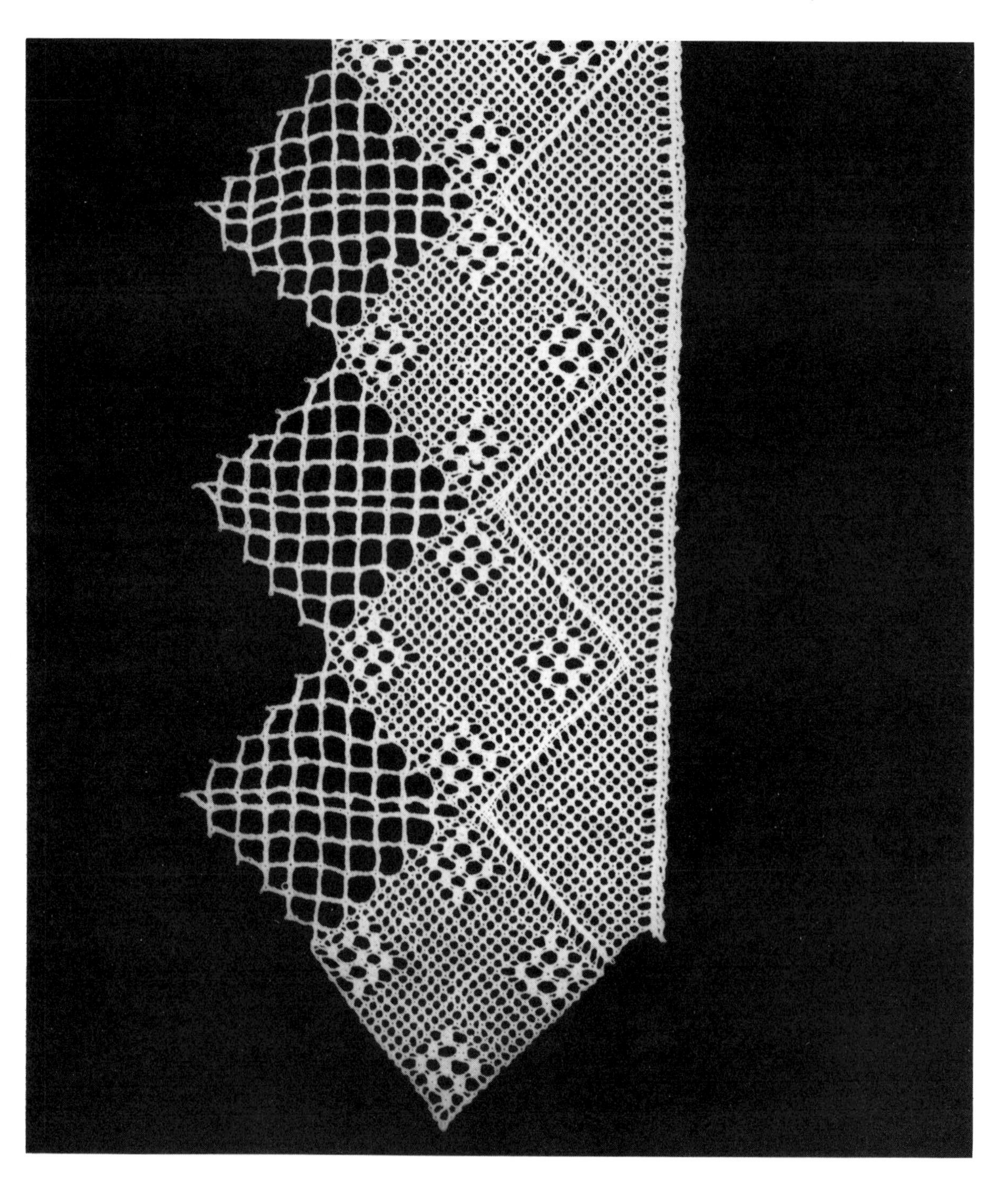

Method of working

Fifty-one pairs are required, plus one extra for the corner. Unless otherwise stated, they are hung on support pins.

Heading 1

1. Hang two pairs open on '**A**'. Do a cloth stitch and twist to cover the pin.
2. The left-hand pair works in cloth stitch through two pairs (passives) to the left. Do a cloth stitch and twist with the next pair; put up pin '**B**'. Cover with a cloth stitch and twist. Work back through passives in cloth stitch, put one twist on the weavers and put the pin up to the left of the two pairs. The footside is now worked as in *PS*, Section I,37.
3. Hang two pairs open on pin '**C**', cover the pin with a cloth stitch and twist. Using the left-hand pair from '**B**' do a half stitch, pin, half stitch, with the right-hand pair from '**C**'.
4. Hang two pairs open on '**D**', cover the pin with a cloth stitch and twist. The left-hand pairs from '**C**' and '**D**' become 'passives' outlining the 'spider motif'.
5. Hang two pairs open on '**E**', cover with a cloth stitch and twist.
6. The right-hand pair from '**E**' works in cloth stitch through two pairs to the right, put on one twist and this pair is now ready to work the Torchon ground.
7. The left-hand pair from '**E**' works a half stitch, pin, half stitch to bring in the 40 pairs hanging on support pins. Let these pairs down immediately.
8. Repeat **6** above for all the next 17 pairs. Now complete the Torchon ground triangle and footsides.
9. The pairs at '**K**' and '**L**' work in cloth stitch through the passives from '**C**' and '**D**' and now become the passives for the 'spider motif'. Put one twist on the passives from '**C**' and '**D**'.
10. Work the 'spider motif', see *BBLS*, page 197.
11. Work the half-stitch plait square. Adjacent pairs from '**T**' to '**V**' are used for the plaits. From '**V**' to '**W**' they are taken in singly for the next 'spider motif'. Where the plaits cross use a two-plait crossing, *PS*, Section IV,24.
12. Corner:
    i) Add one pair at '**M**' to work the line of ground to '**N**'.
    ii) This pair work as a passive pair from '**N**' to '**P**'.
    iii) At '**P**' this pair will become part of the half-stitch plait working to '**R**'.
    iv) Complete the plait to '**S**'. Here the extra pair becomes a passive again until the end of the motif where it may be discarded.

Heading 2

1. The pairs are hung on open as indicated in the diagram.
2. Where four pairs are hung on, work left-hand pairs through right hand in cloth stitch. These are now ready to work the spiders.
3. Where two pairs are hung on, cover with a cloth stitch and twist except for the passive pairs at the footside.
4. Where three pairs are hung on open, work left-hand pair in cloth stitch through to the right. Left-hand two pairs become half stitch plait; right-hand pair has one twist added and will work in half stitch, pin, half stitch to complete the 'spider motif'.
5. Work as for Heading 1.

NB: This heading is to be used for curtain blinds, etc., and the edge may be strengthened by sewing on to a narrow ribbon or petersham.

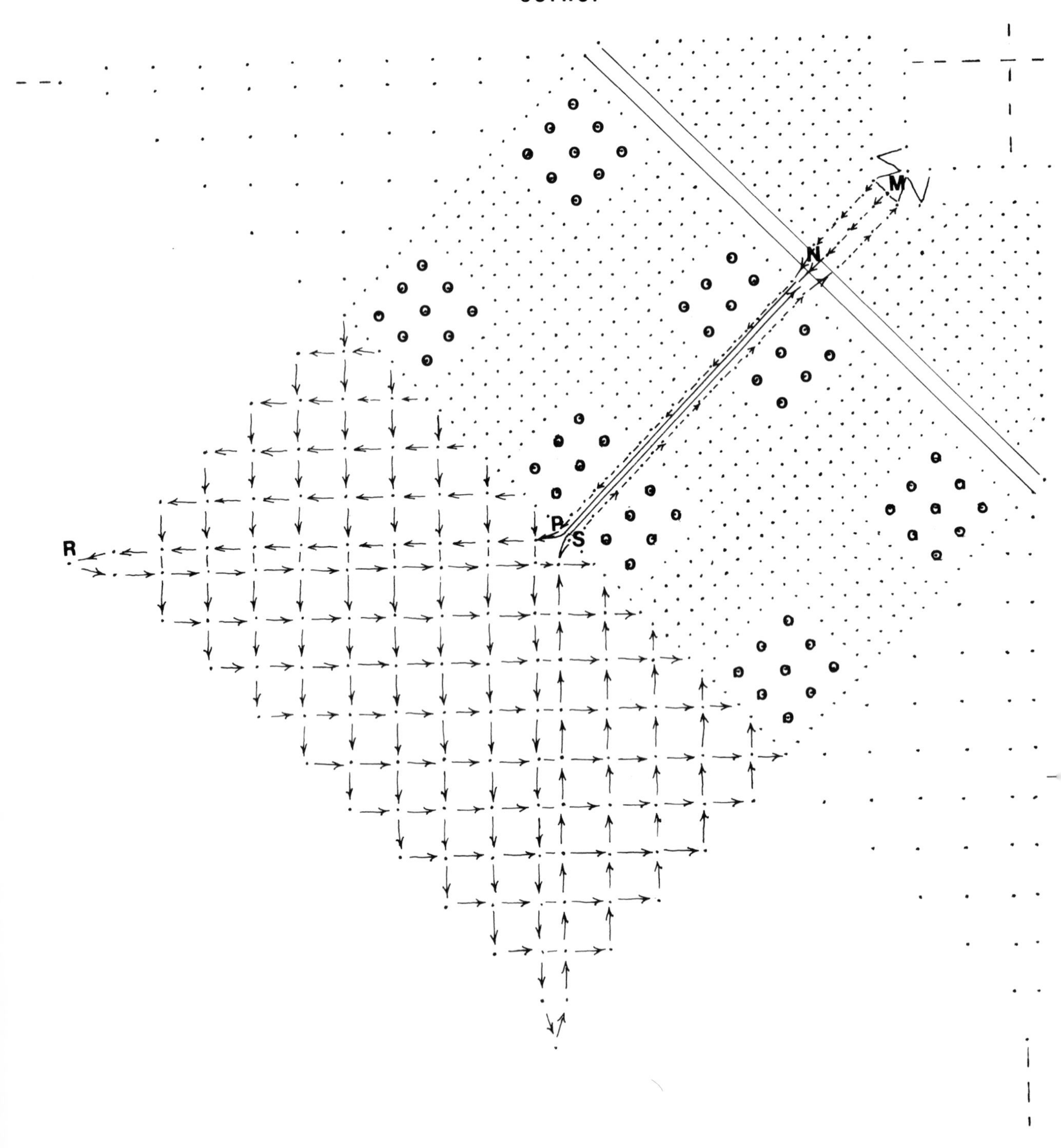
corner
M
N
P
S
R

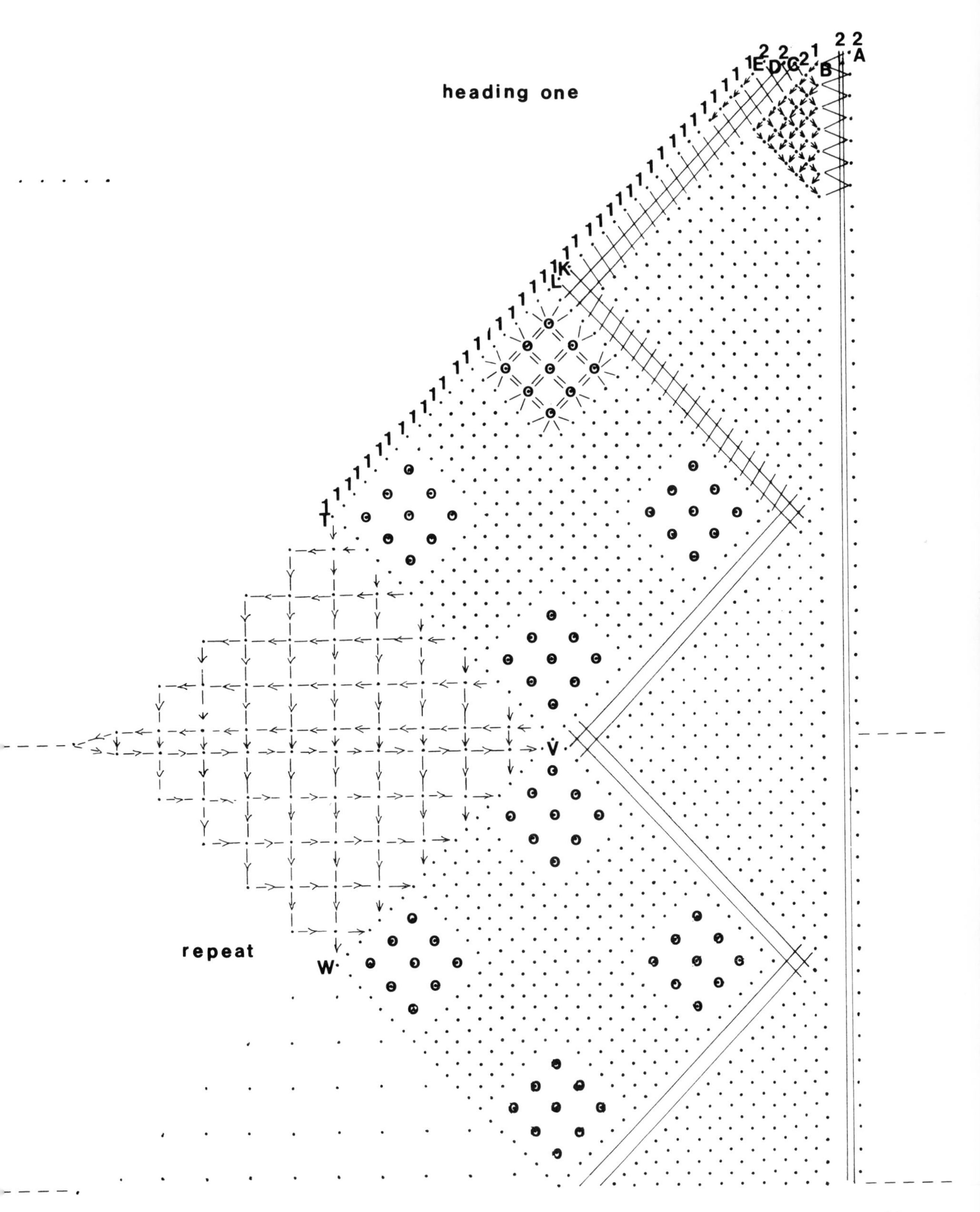
heading one
A
B
C
D
E
K
L
T
V
W
repeat

heading two

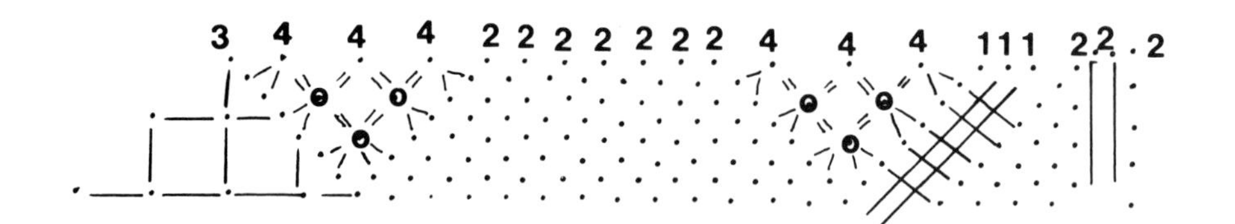

Spring (snowdrops)

Madiera Tanne 50

This and the following three patterns illustrate the four seasons and are designed for framing.

Method of working

See *PS* Section VI, 24 for 'ten-stick', which is worked using five pairs.

Leaves

1. Three pairs are hung on open. Increase to nine pairs.
2. These may be worked in cloth stitch or half stitch. In the latter case do cloth stitch and twist at the footside.

Snowdrops

1. Work the stalks first and carry these pairs into the calyx at the top of the flower. The thicker stalks are worked as 'ten-sticks', the thinner as half stitch plaits.
2. The pairs that have been used to work the calyx are then used to work the petals, extra pairs being added to keep the density even. Twists may be used on the weavers to vary the appearance of the cloth stitch petals.
3. Flower and calyx footsides – see *PS* Section I, 37.

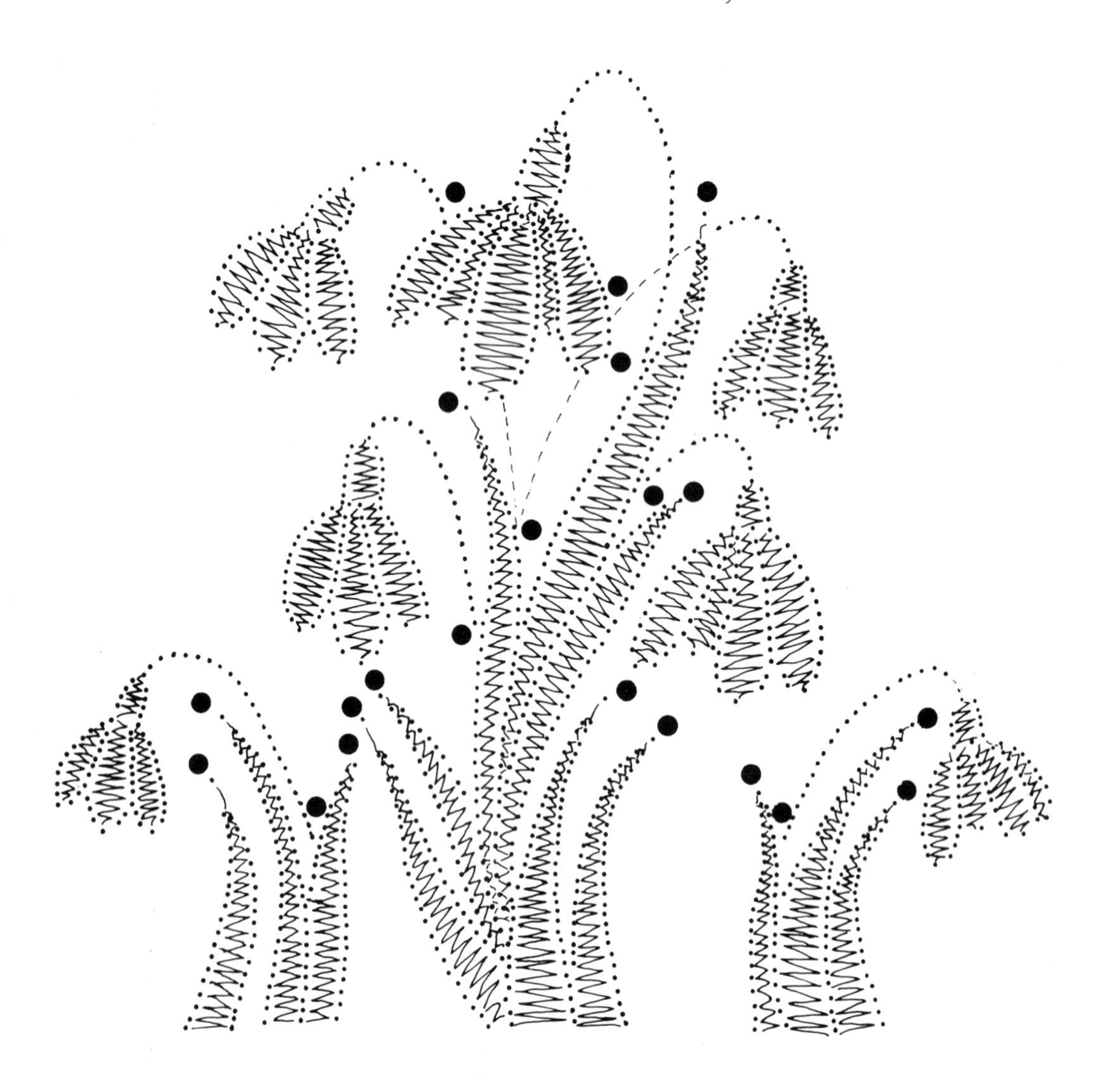

Summer (strawberries)

Madiera Tanne 50
DMC Coton perlé 5

Method of working

Leaves

These are worked in cloth stitch with a single gimp thread as the centre vein. For numbers 1, 3 and 5, finish off as in *PS* Section IX, 33.

1. Leaf 1: hang on five pairs, increase to eight pairs plus a single gimp. Decrease to five pairs at the bottom and then increase for the second leaf. Footsides as in *PS* Section I, 37.
2. Leaf 2: hang on five pairs, increase to eight pairs plus a single gimp.
3. Leaf 3: hang on five pairs, increase to nine pairs plus a single gimp.
4. Leaves 4 and 5: hang on five pairs, increase to eleven pairs plus a single gimp. Decrease to five pairs and then increase for second leaf. Three pairs are left off at the base of the first leaf to work the stalk from 'a'.

Strawberries

1 Work the small leaves first in half stitch. Hang on four pairs and add more as necessary. The pairs from the leaves are then used to work the berry.

2. The textured appearance is achieved by adding a twist on the weavers at random in the cloth stitch.

Flower (No. 8)

1. Base (calyx): hang on four pairs, increase to eight pairs. Work in cloth stitch.
2. Petals: hang on eight pairs and work in half stitch.

Stalks

Use three or four pairs and work in cloth stitch.

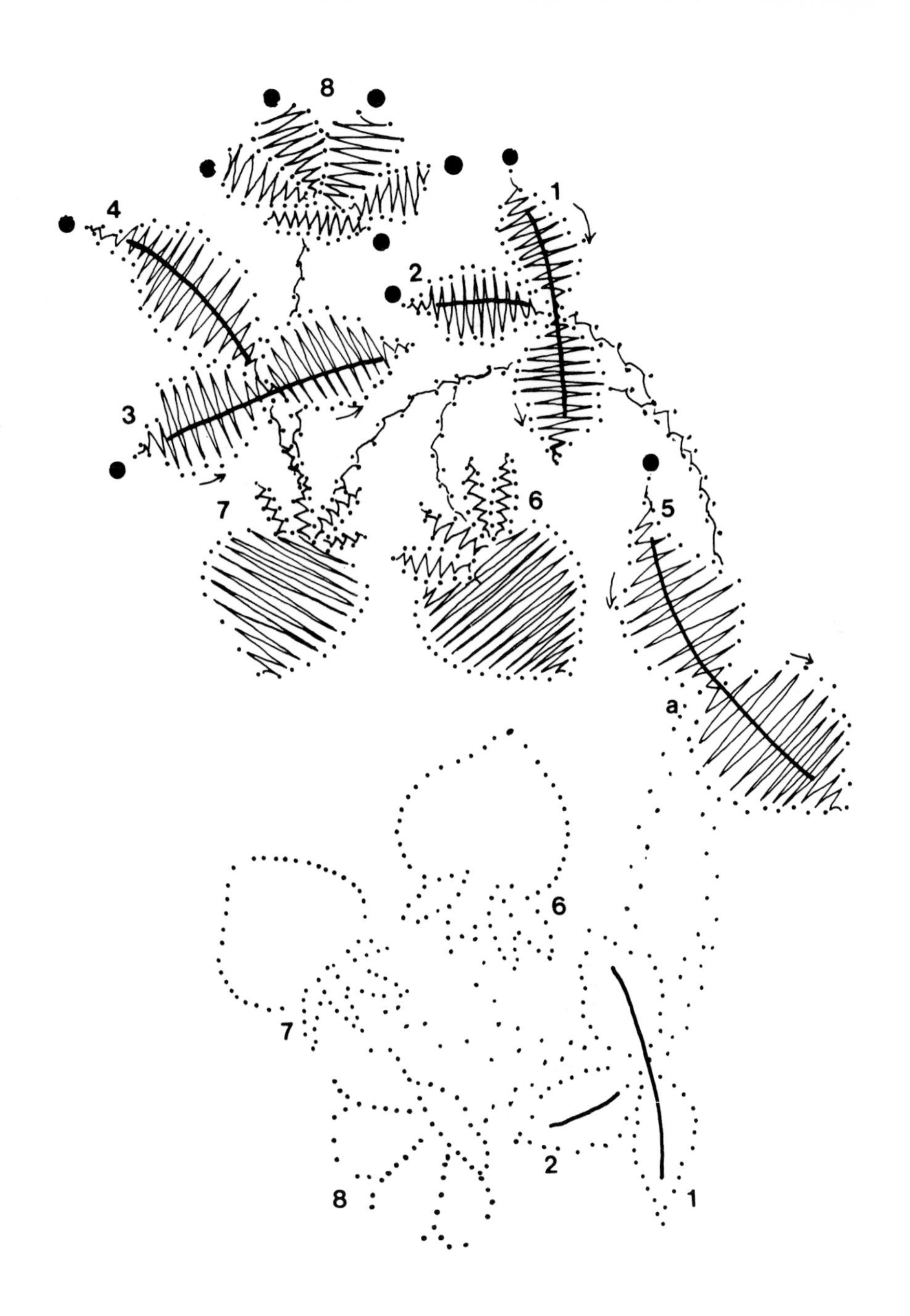
8
4
1
2
3
7
6
5
a
6
7
2
8
1

Autumn (barley ears)

Brok 100

Method of working

The order of work is **A** to **N**.

Barley ears

1. Commence at the base of each stalk with four pairs. Work in cloth stitch and then use these pairs for the 'ten-stick' in which ears are worked. Working in a circular path, complete the bottom set.
2. Where the second set of ears joins the first set, bring in four pairs as the first ear is worked. Put them to one side until the first set has been completed. Now complete the second set, again bringing in pairs for the next set to be worked. Repeat until all the ears have been worked.
3. The centre vein is one twisted pair worked from the top.
4. The 'hairs' are single twisted pairs.

Leaves

These are worked either in cloth stitch or half stitch, using four to six pairs as necessary.

Side shoots

Where these occur on the stalks, use two or three pairs and work in cloth stitch.

NB: In second illustration, half stitch plaits have been used instead of 'ten-stick', and it can be seen that the design now resembles coral rather than barley.

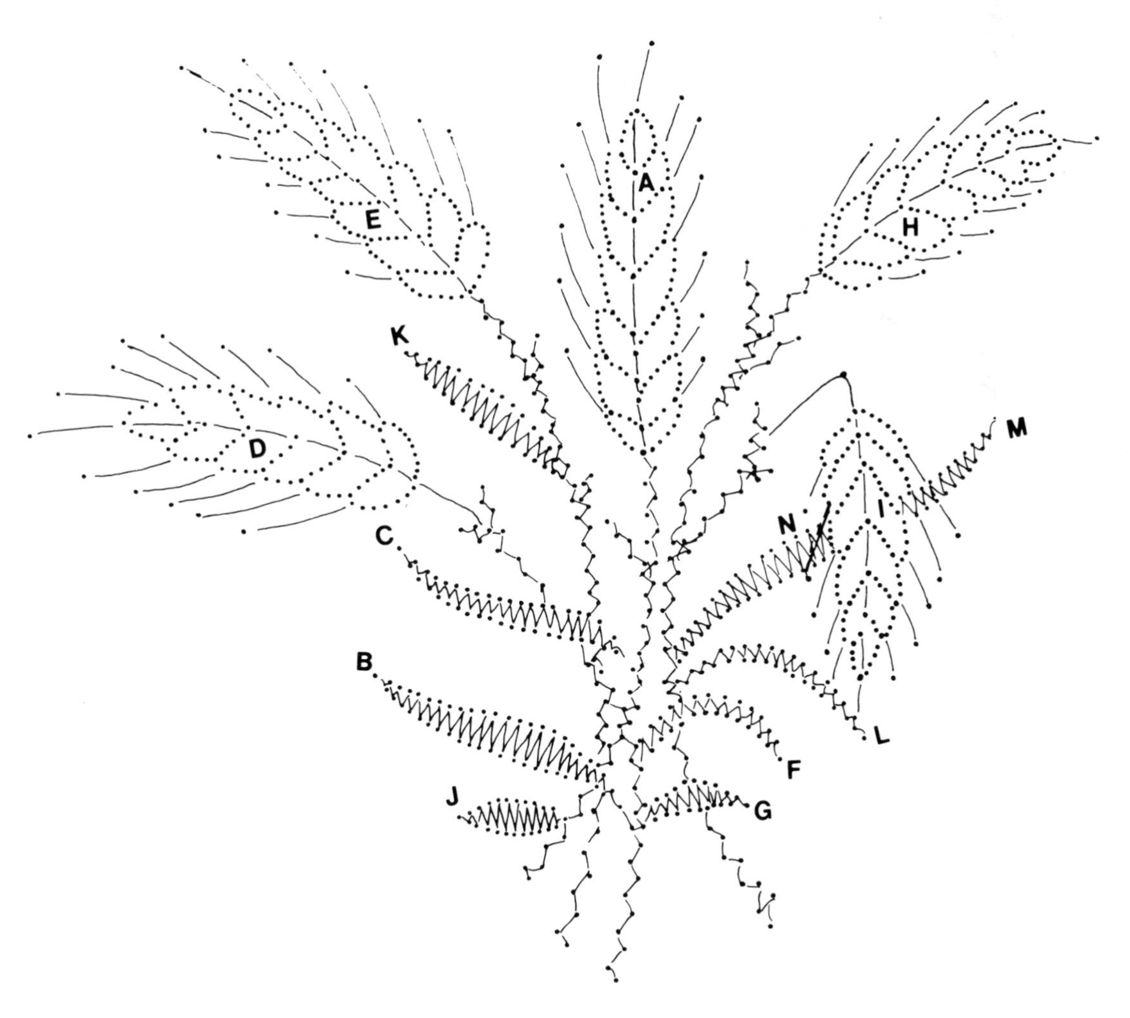

Winter (holly leaves)

Brok 100
DMC Coton perlé 5

Method of Working

The leaves are worked 1 to 8 in order and the directions are all as for leaf 1. The larger ones have a single gimp thread as the centre vein.

Leaves

1. Leaf 1: hang on two pairs and increase to seven pairs, increasing and decreasing as necessary for the shape. Work in cloth stitch decreasing to three pairs which are used to work the stalk.
2. Leaf 2: hang on two pairs and increase to five pairs.
3. Leaves 3, 4 and 8: hang on four pairs and increase to fourteen pairs.
4. Leaf 5: hang on three pairs, increase to fourteen pairs and then reduce to three pairs for the stalk.
5. Leaves 6 and 7: hang on three pairs, increase to seventeen pairs and reduce to three pairs for the stalk.

Berries

1. Work in half stitch using five or six pairs, depending on size.
2. The stalks are worked as half stitch plaits.
3. Berries **A** and **B** are worked using the pairs forming the stalk.

Galaxy

Bockens 50

This may be used as a mat, window hanging, or a picture.

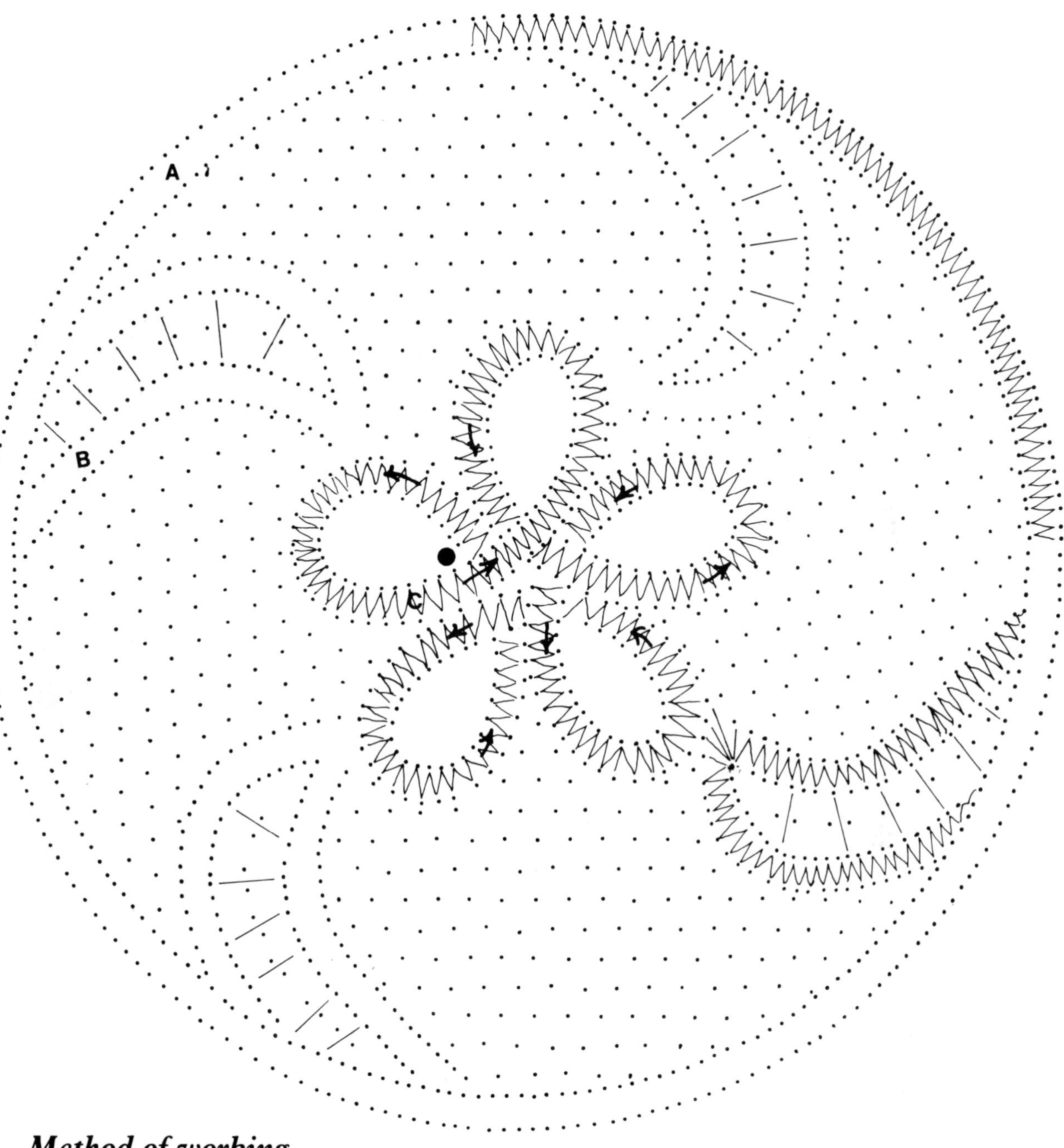

Method of working

Outer trail A

Use six pairs and start as in *PS*, Section I, 6, using cloth stitch and twist footsides.

Trail(s) B

1. These have each been worked differently to show the effect of using different stitches in the same pricking.
2. Half stitch plaits and picots have been used for joining the trail.

Trail C

Using six pairs, hang on as for Trail A and work in cloth stitch.

Filling

Use point ground or an alternative if desired.

Spider's web

Bockens 60

This may be used as a window-hanging decoration or a picture.

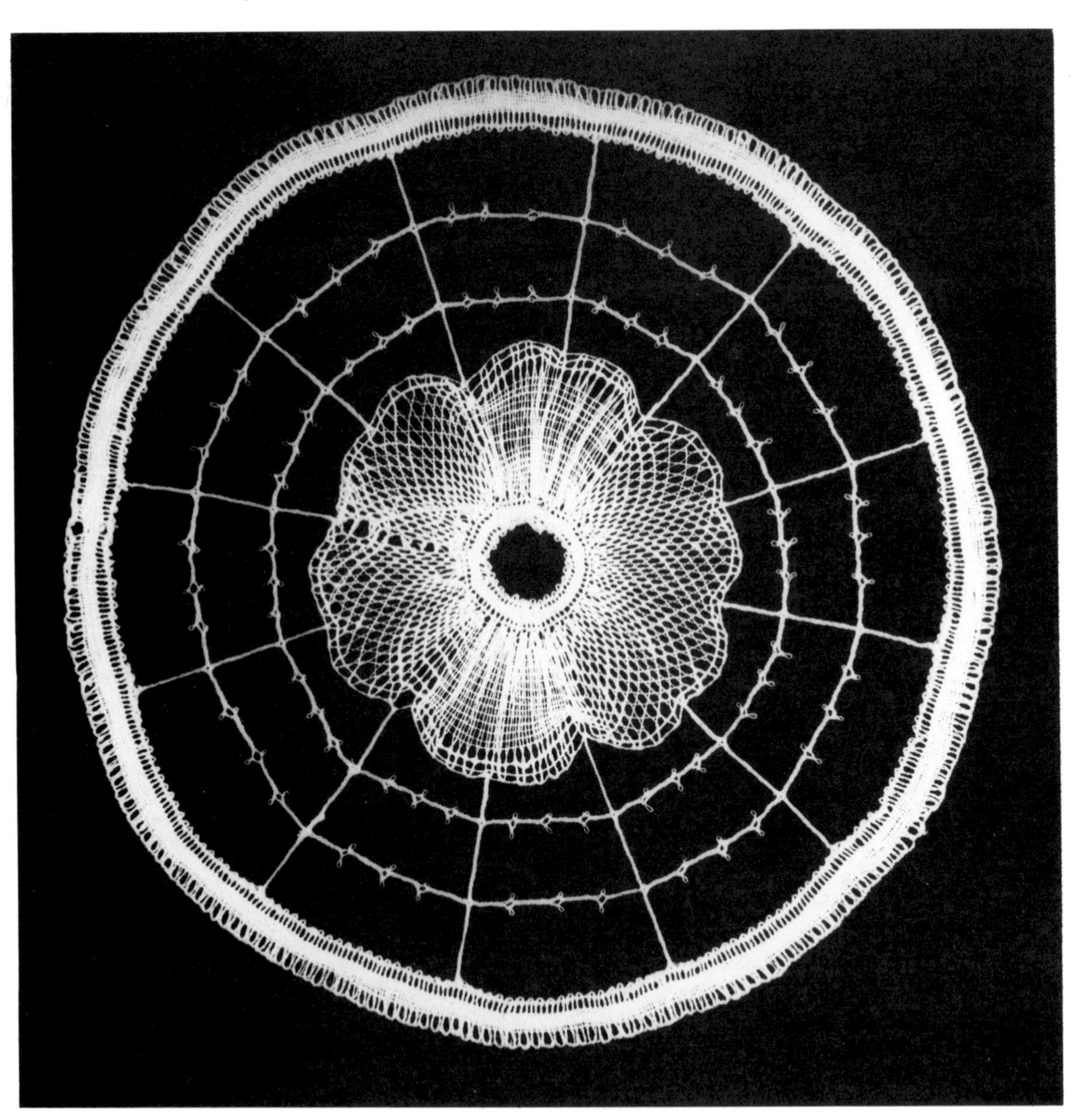

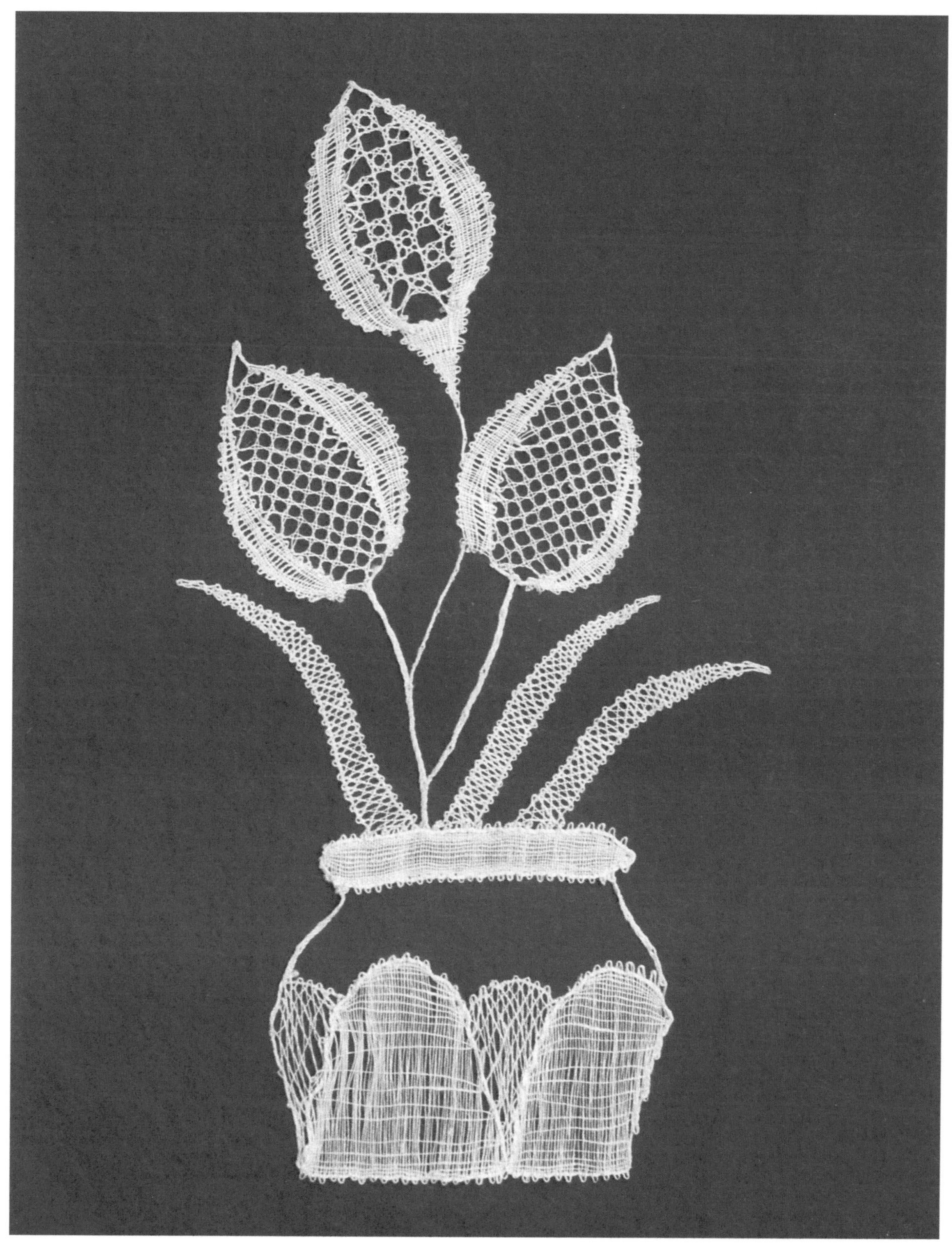

Tulips

Fan

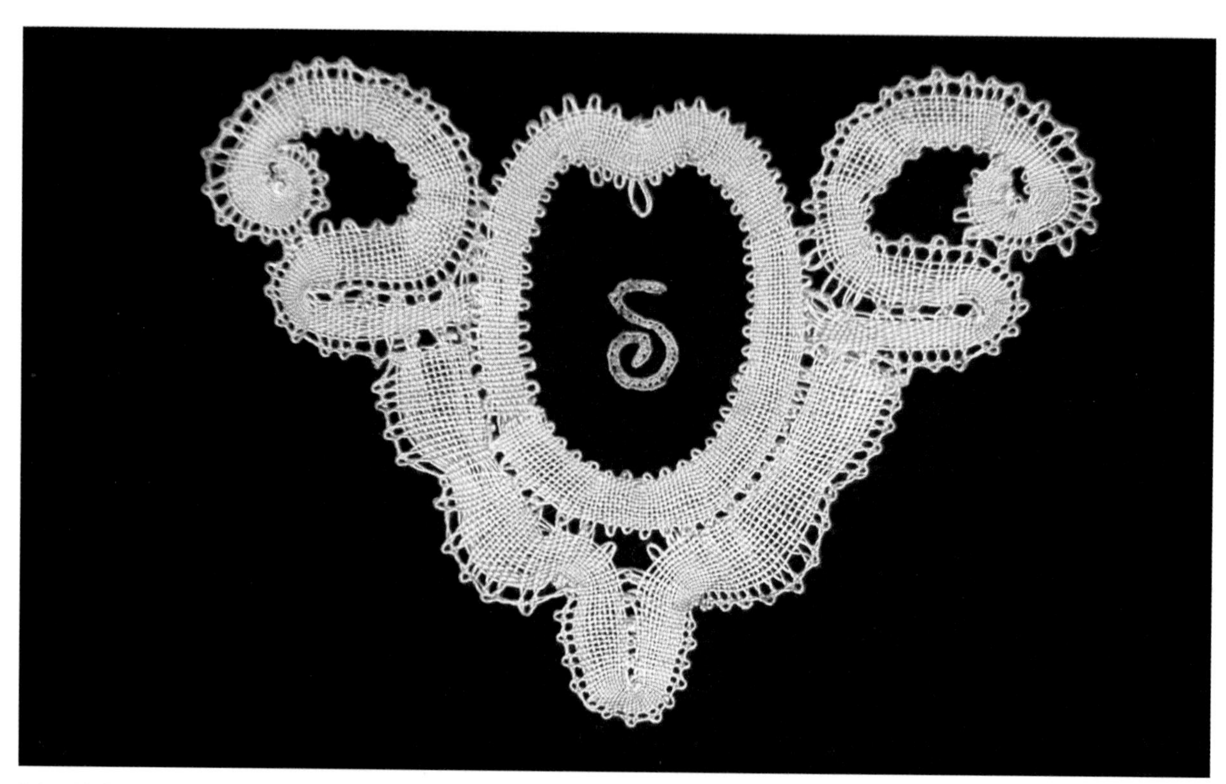

Motif 3

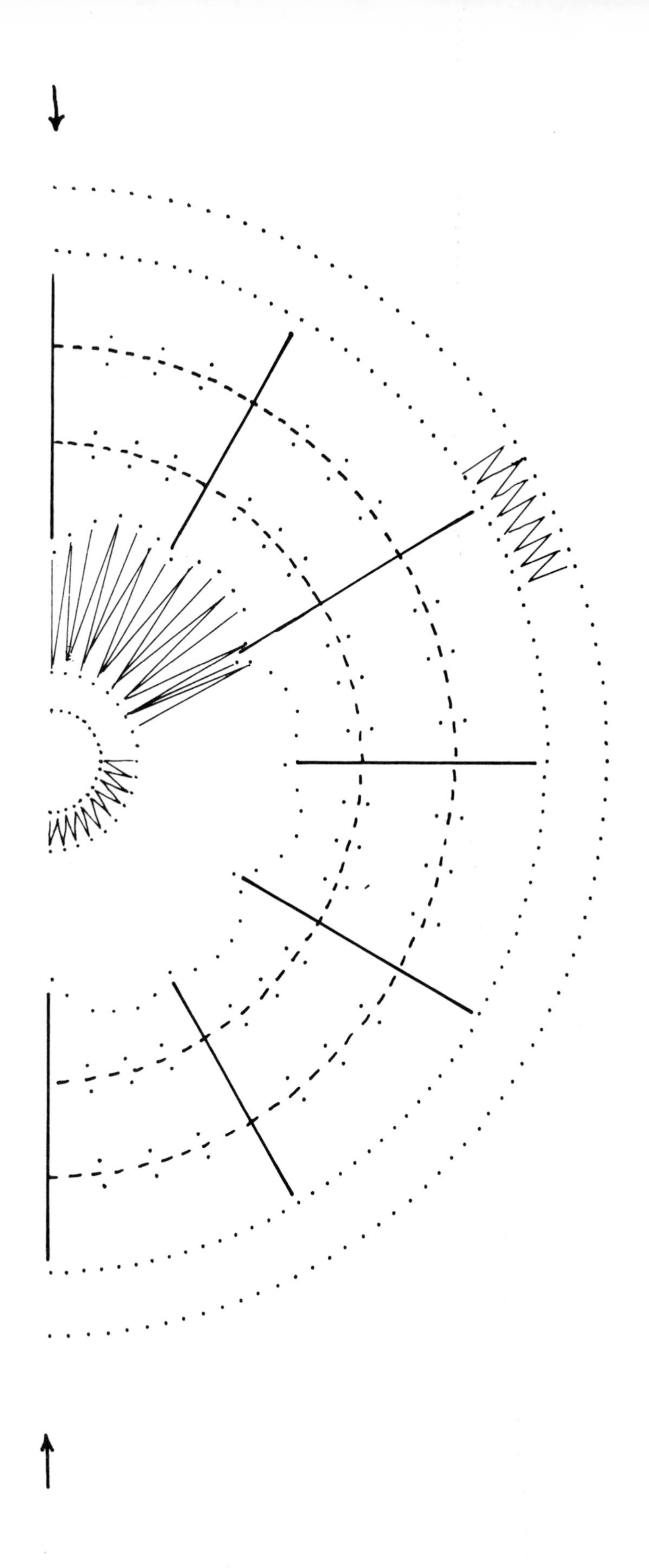

Method of Working

Outer trail

1. Hang on seven pairs as in *PS*, Section I, 6.
2. The outer footside is worked as in *PS*, Section 1, 37. The inner footside is in cloth stitch and twist.

Flower

This is worked in *BFL* pages 64–5 technique using ten pairs for the petals and five pairs for the inner ring.

Spokes

These are worked as half stitch plaits and picots.

Animal motifs

Madiera tanne 30

These may be used as pictures for children, or as motifs to decorate clothing.

Method of Working

Rabbit

1. **Hem of skirt**
   i) Hang on seven pairs as in *PS*, Section I, 6.
   ii) Work in cloth stitch with cloth stitch and twist footsides.
   iii) To finish, reverse instructions for start.

2. **Ears, face and arms**
   i) Hang on five pairs at top of ears, work in cloth stitch, with footsides as in *PS*, Section I, 37.
   ii) The weavers from the ears meet at '**A**' in cloth stitch.
   iii) Continue in cloth stitch: add one pair on each side at '**B**'.
   iv) Complete the face, decreasing for the chin.
   v) Add one pair at '**C**'. Using pairs from the face, work the arm at the same time as finishing off the face (four pairs in total for the arms).

3. **Skirt**
   i) Eight pairs are hung on along the chin and a further eight pairs at the arms.
   ii) Work in half stitch, and bow in to hem.

4. **Eyes** – these may be french knots, beads, etc.

5. **Whiskers and nose** – embroider these.

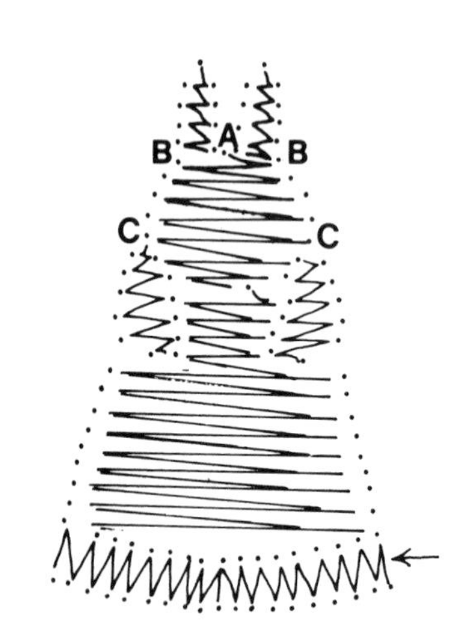

Ducklings

NB: Footsides for the face, neck and straight leg are as in Rabbit 2.i.

1. **Face**
   i) Hang on five pairs, work in cloth stitch, increasing to fourteen pairs.
   ii) Work the feathers in half stitch plaits and picots.
2. **Raised foot** – hang on five pairs and work in half stitch.
3. **Trousers**
   i) Hang on six pairs, work in cloth stitch with cloth stitch and twist footsides.
   ii) Carry pairs over the raised foot for use in the next trouser leg.
4. **Skirt**
   i) Hang on five pairs and increase to fourteen pairs.
   ii) Work in cloth stitch, twists being added to give a textured effect.
5. **Blouse** – hang on eight pairs, increase to fourteen pairs, and work in half stitch.
6. **Leg** – hang on four pairs, increase to six pairs for foot and work in cloth stitch.
7. **Neck** – hang on eight pairs, work in cloth stitch.
8. **Eyes** – as for Rabbit.

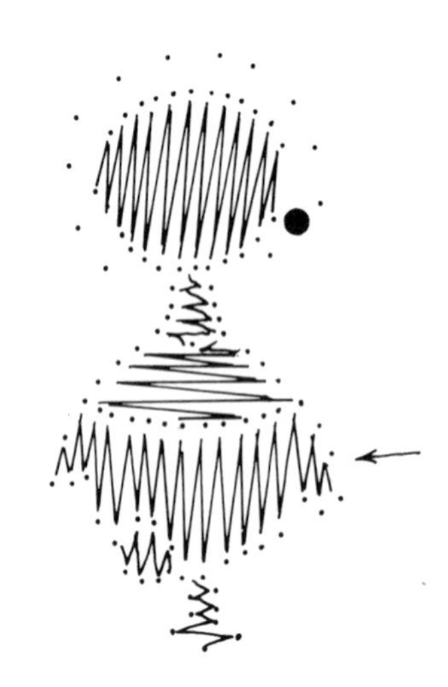

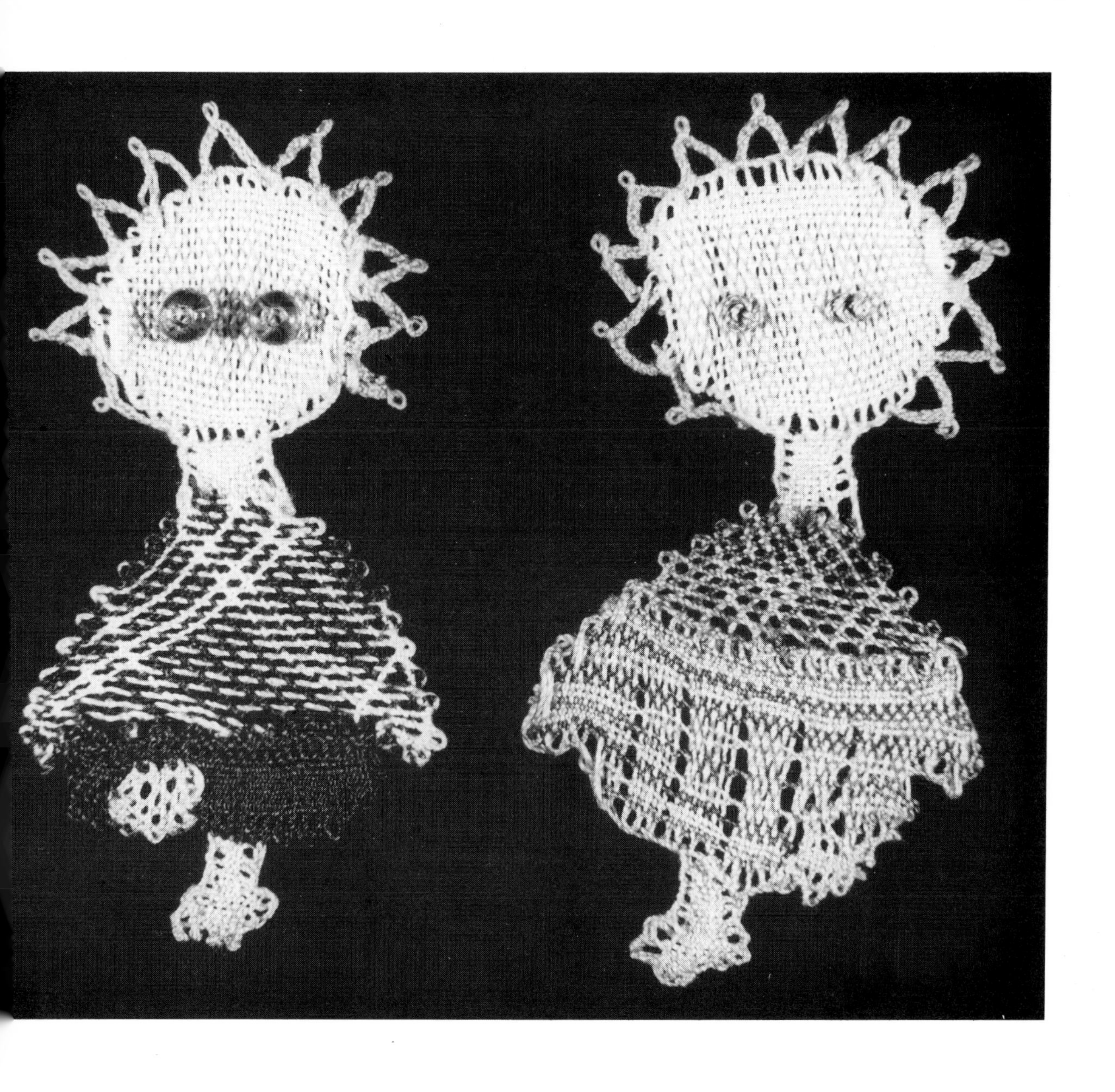

Teddy bears

1. **Face** – hang on four pairs, increase to eleven pairs and work as Rabbit 2.i.
2. **Ears**
   i) Hang on four pairs and increase to eight pairs.
   ii) Work in half stitch.
3. **Dress**
   i) Hang on six pairs, increase to thirteen pairs. Work top in half stitch.
   ii) Work the skirt in cloth stitch with twists on the weavers for texturing.
4. **Frill**
   i) Hang on four pairs, increase to six pairs.
   ii) Work in half stitch.
5. **Trousers and legs**
   i) Hang on four pairs and increase to eight pairs, work in cloth stitch.
   ii) Join the weavers at '**F**' and work the trousers.
6. **Arms** – hang on five or six pairs, work in half stitch.
7. **Neck** – hang on seven pairs, work in cloth stitch.
8. **Eyes** – as for Rabbit.

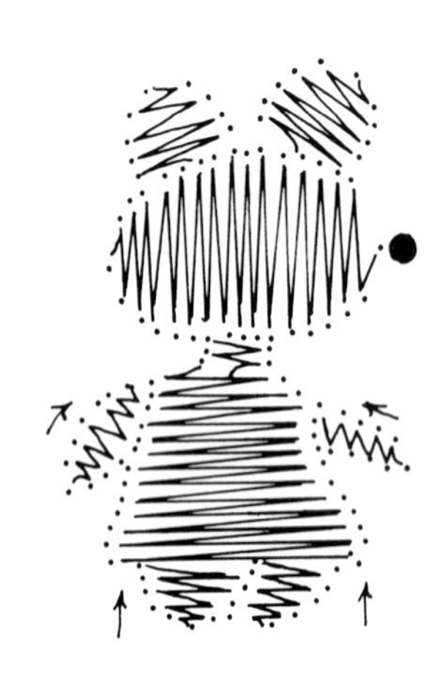

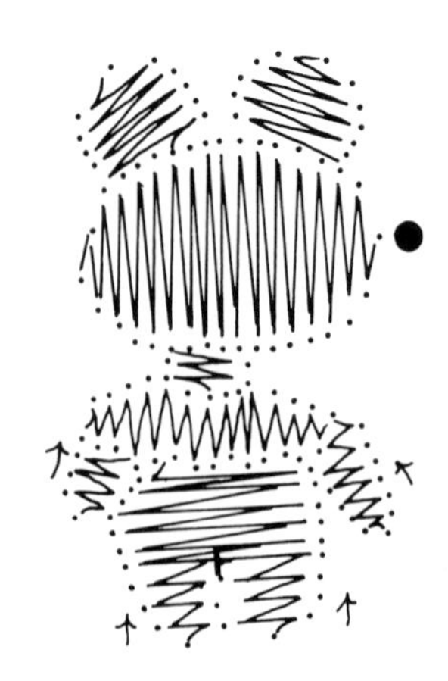

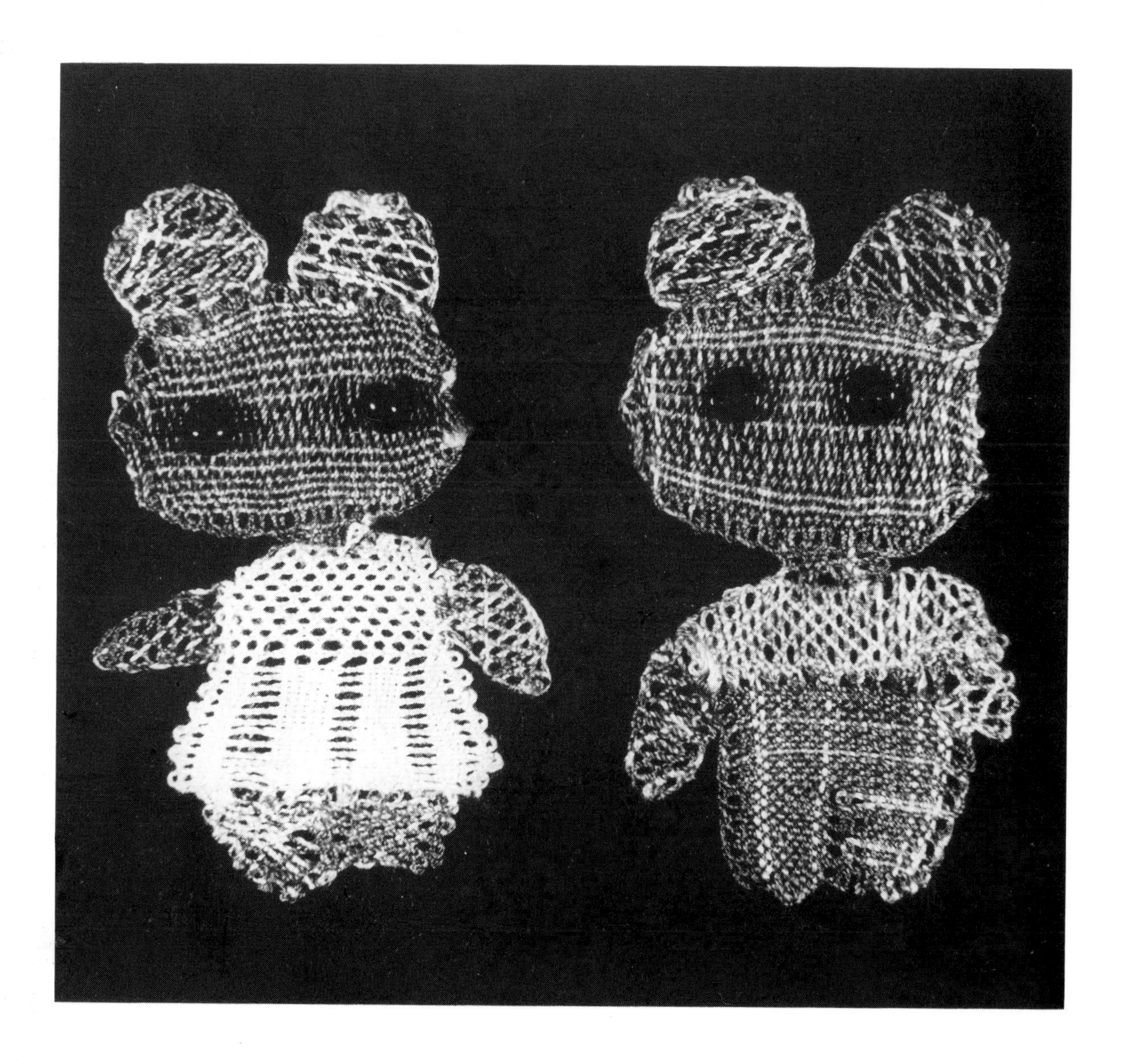

Kitten

1. **Dress**
   i) Hang on three pairs at each shoulder, work in cloth stitch.
   ii) Add four pairs across the neck.
   iii) Work the skirt in half stitch, adding pairs to a total of thirteen.
2. **Ears and face**
   i) Hang on five pairs at the tops of the ears. Work as Rabbit 2.i.
   ii) The weaver from the left-hand ear ('**G**') works through five pairs (on support pins) for the forehead and then through the pairs from the right-hand ear.
   iii) Complete the face in cloth stitch.
3. **Arms** – hang on four or five pairs, work in cloth stitch.
4. **Tail/foot** – hang on five pairs at '**H**', work in cloth stitch.
5. **Leg** – hang on six pairs, work in cloth stitch.
6. **Whiskers/nose** – embroider these.

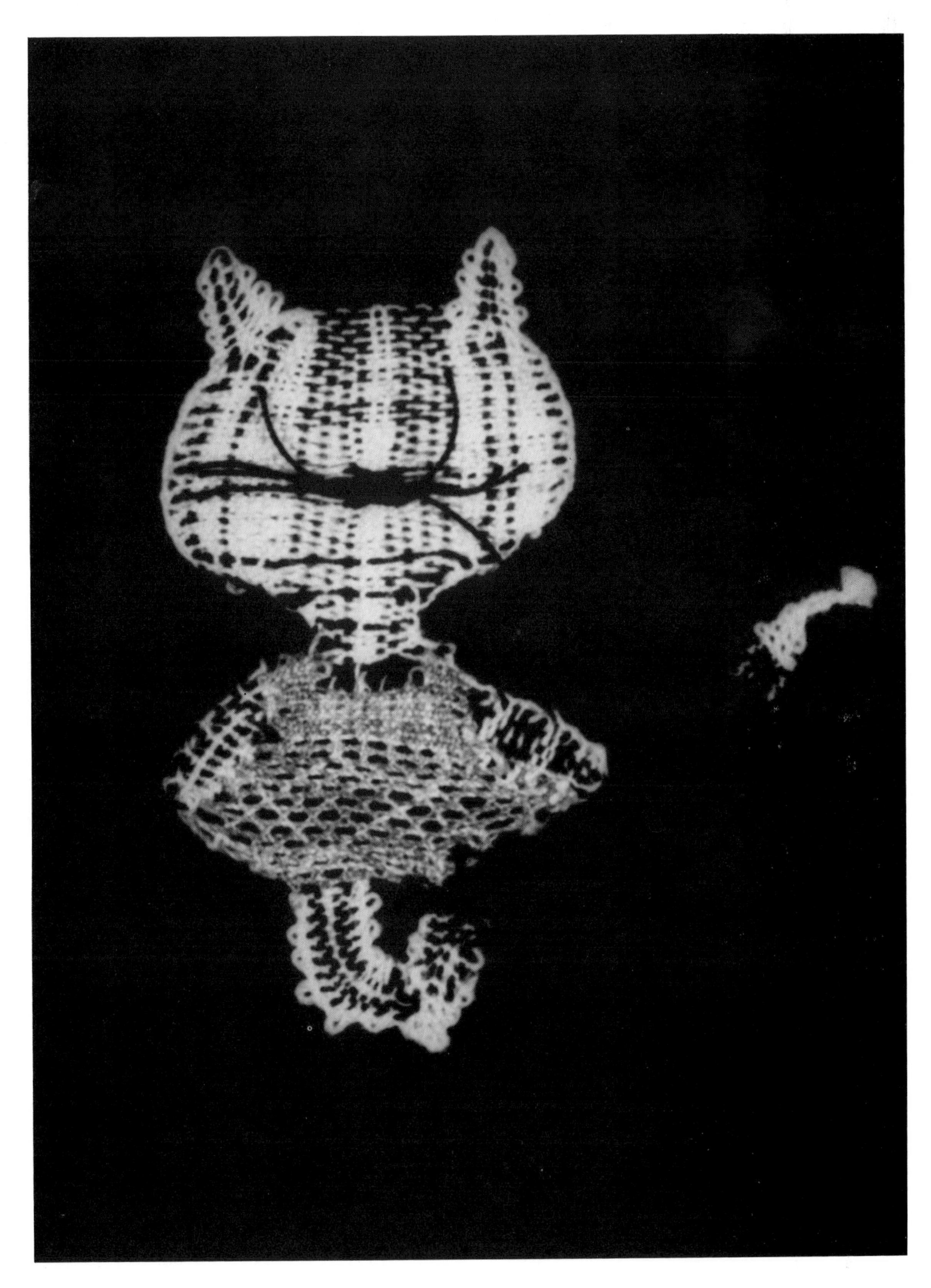

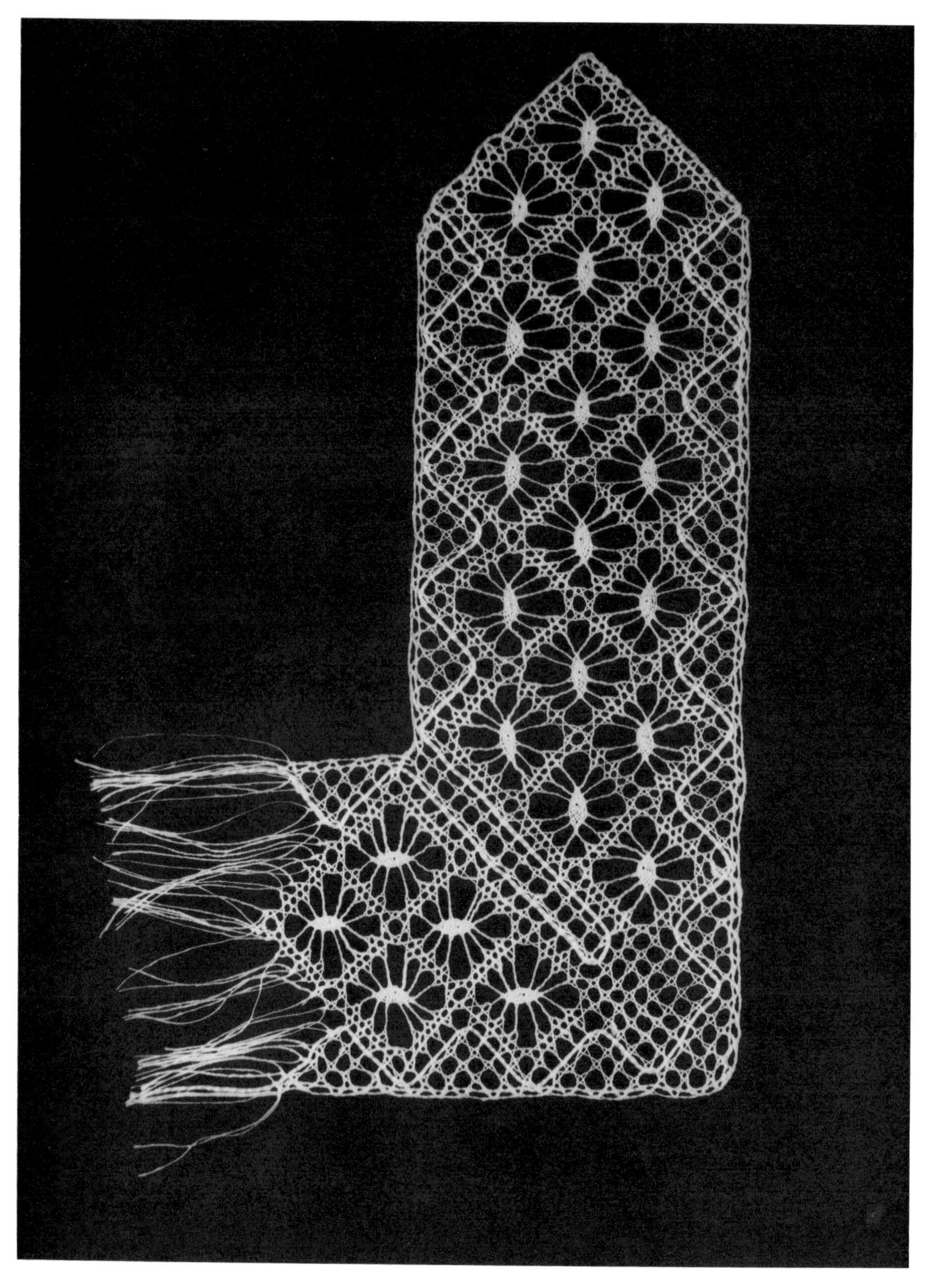

Edging 1

BOUC fil de lin dentelle 100/2
DMC Coton perlé 8, 28 pairs, one gimp pair

This design, together with the following two, has been adapted from patterns used by Mrs Ann Grugeon (1859–1946) who lived in Finchingfield, Essex. Her grandson, Noel Choat, very kindly allowed me to see her patterns and also her pillow (of very elementary French design – the roller being stuffed with wool!) and it seems she used a mixture of coarse French and English bobbins.

Method of Working

1. Hang two pairs open on '**A**'. Hang the other pairs on support pins. Take the gimp through eleven pairs on each side of '**A**', including the pairs hanging on '**A**'.
2. Work as *BBLS*, page 219.
3. A spider is worked in the corner. (This could also be a tally or Torchon ground.)
4. Footsides:
   i) Using three pairs and working from the centre of the work to the outside edge, do a cloth stitch and twist with two pairs. Put an extra twist on the outer pair.
   ii) Put the pin up between the second and third pairs from the outside edge and cover with a cloth stitch and twist.

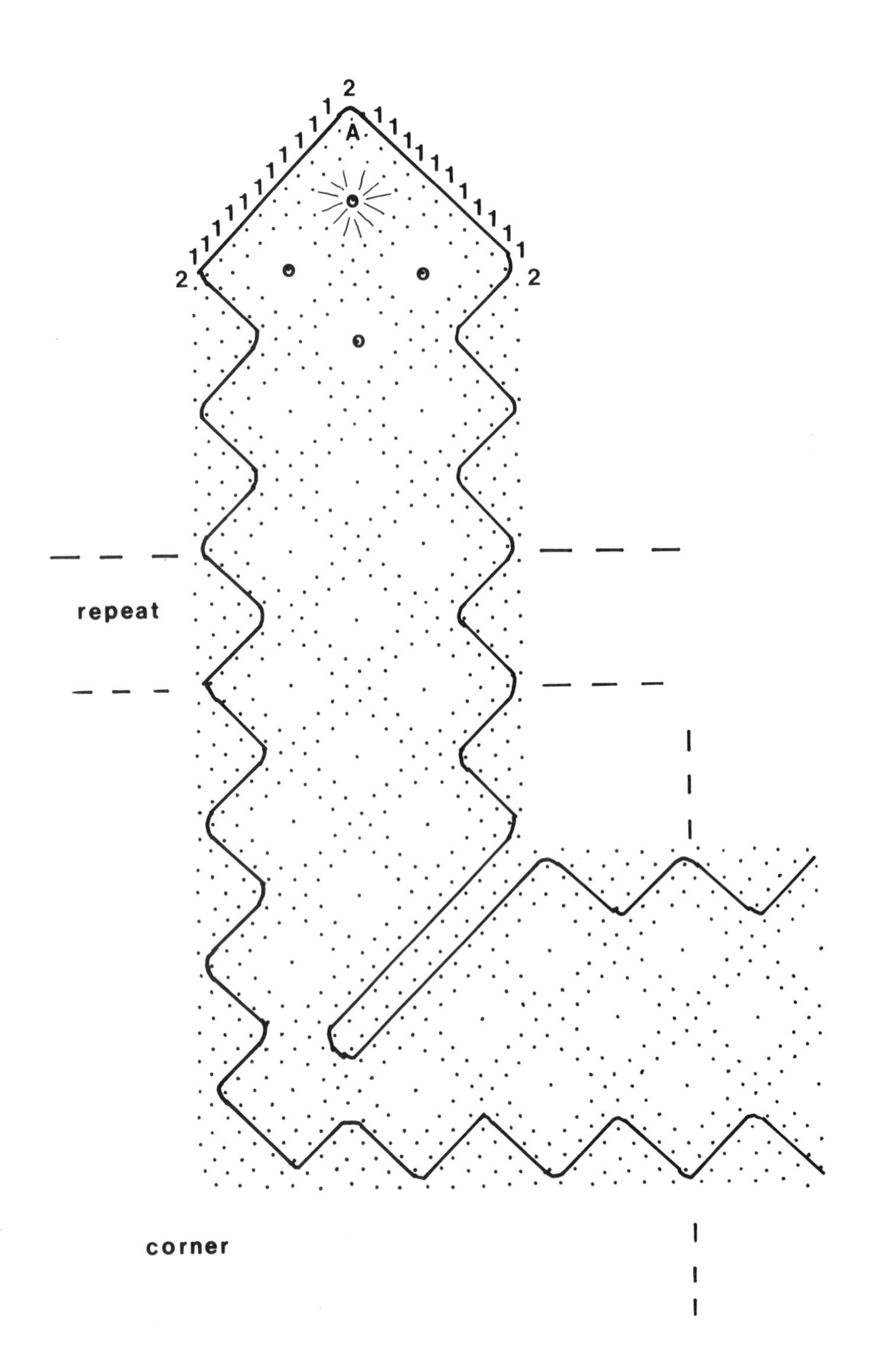
2
A
1 1 1 1 1 1 1 1 1 1 1 1 1 1 1 1 1
2
2
repeat
corner

Edging 2

BOUC fil de lin dentelle 100/2
34 pairs

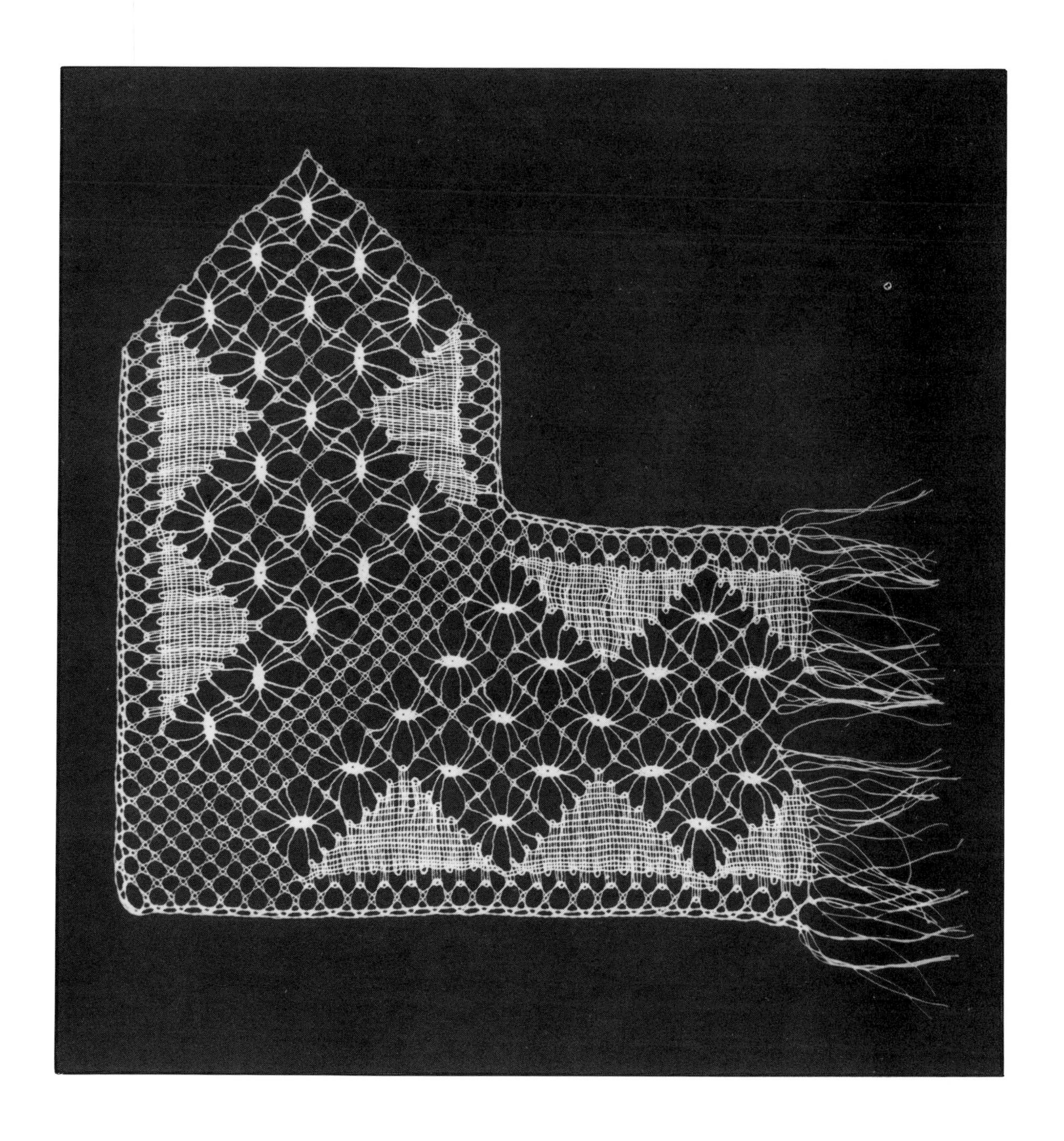

Method of working

1. Hang two pairs open on '**A**', cover with a cloth stitch and twist.
2. Hang the next 28 pairs evenly on support pins on either side. Work in half stitch, pin, half stitch. Let each pair down as the pin is covered.
3. Work the first eight 'spiders'.
4. The last two pairs on each side are hung open on a support pin. Work a footside stitch as in the previous pattern.
5. The cloth stitch triangle may now be worked.
6. The corner may be worked as shown in Torchon ground, or as suggested for Edging 1.

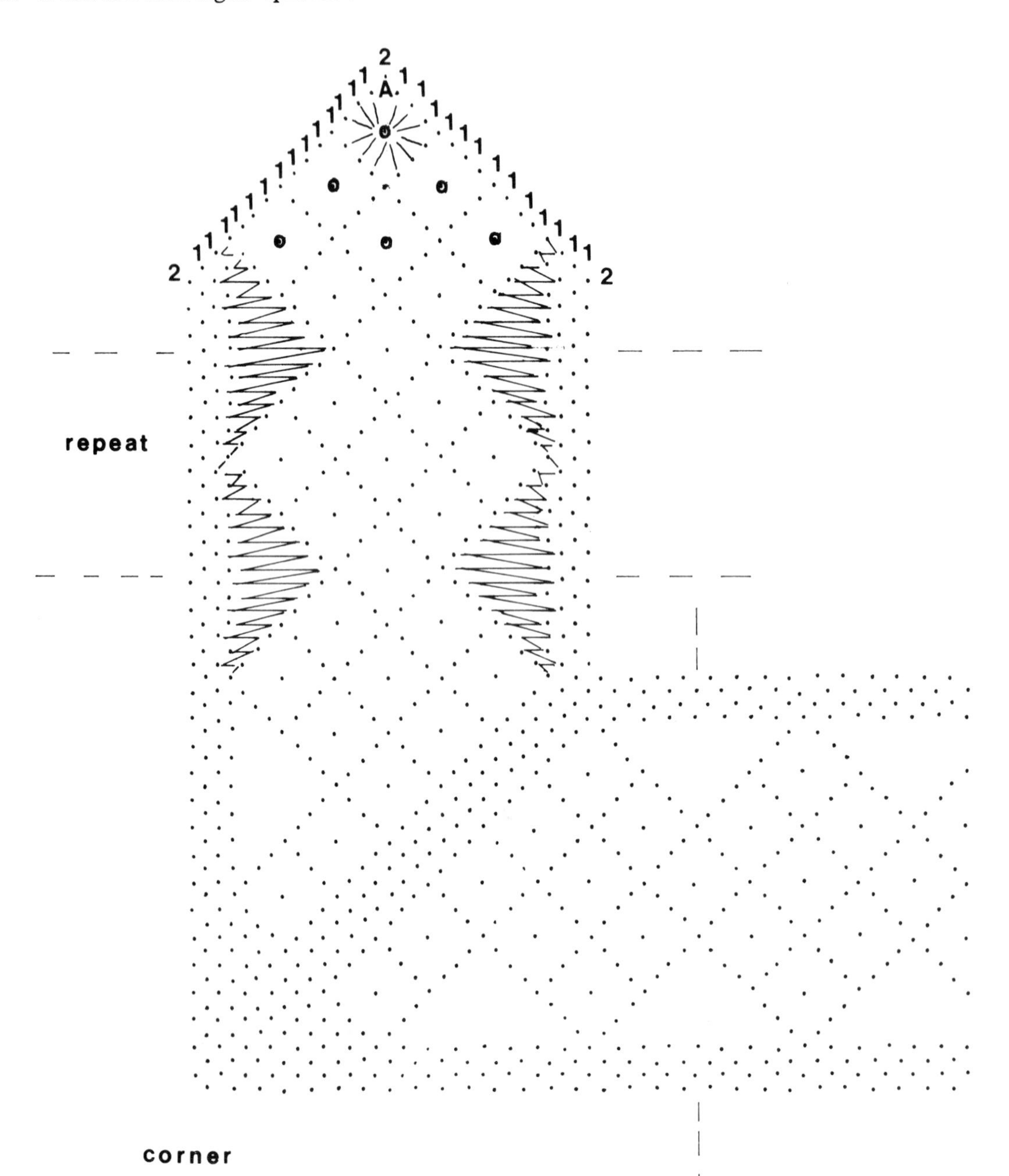

Animal motifs

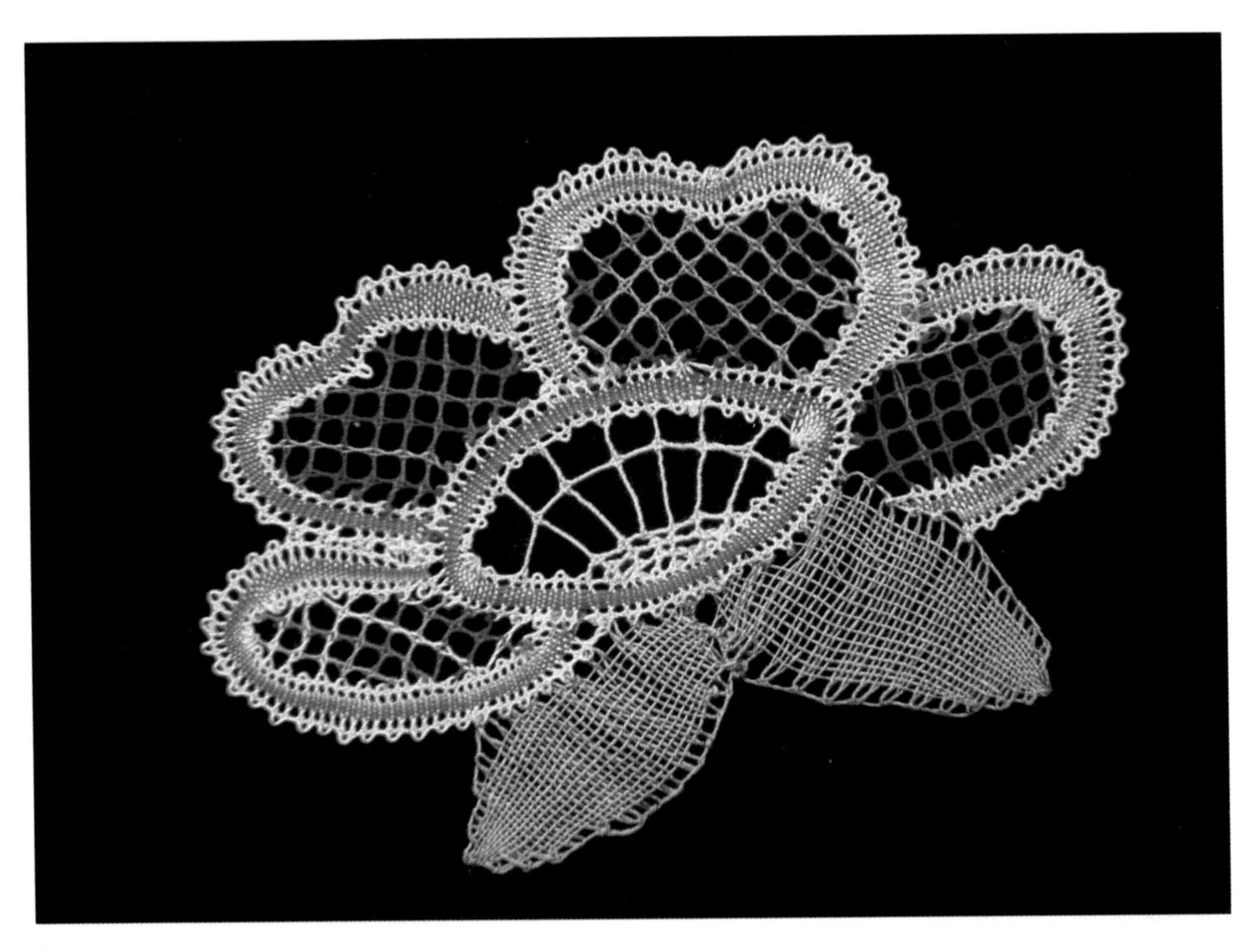

Rose

Sunburst

Bridge coasters

Edging 3

BOUC fil de lin dentelle 100/2
18 pairs

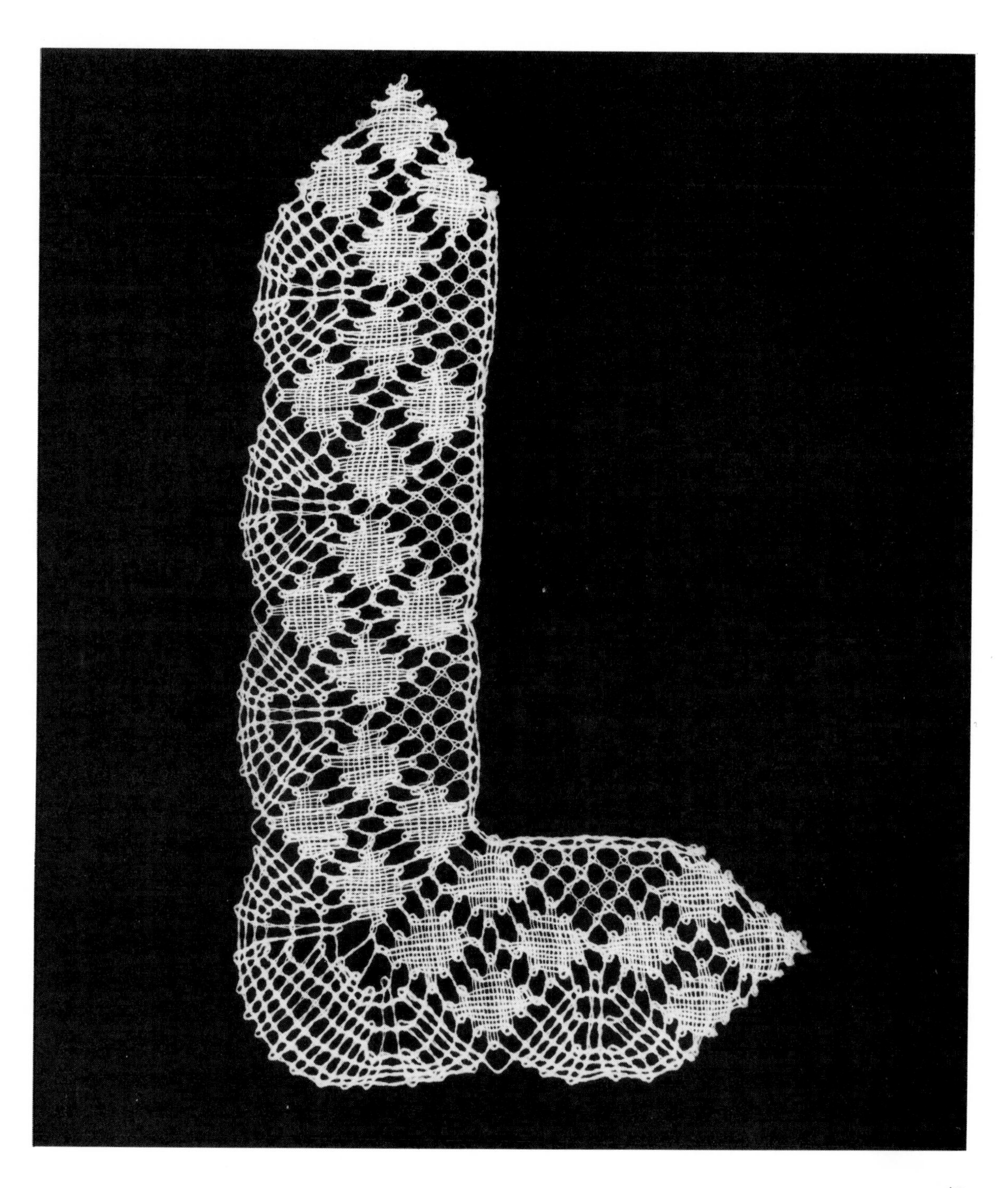

Method of working

1. Hang two pairs open at '**A**'. The next six pairs on either side are on support pins.
2. Work the first cloth stitch diamond. Leave the pairs on the support pins until the diamond is finished, then pull them evenly down.
3. At '**B**', two pairs are brought in to work the footside (see Edging 1).
4. At '**C**', two pairs are brought in to work the headside. One pair becomes a passive, the other the weaver. The headside has been worked in cloth stitch and twist, but it could be in cloth stitch or with one thicker thread as the weaver.
5. The cloth stitch diamonds could also be varied, i.e. spiders, half stitch etc.

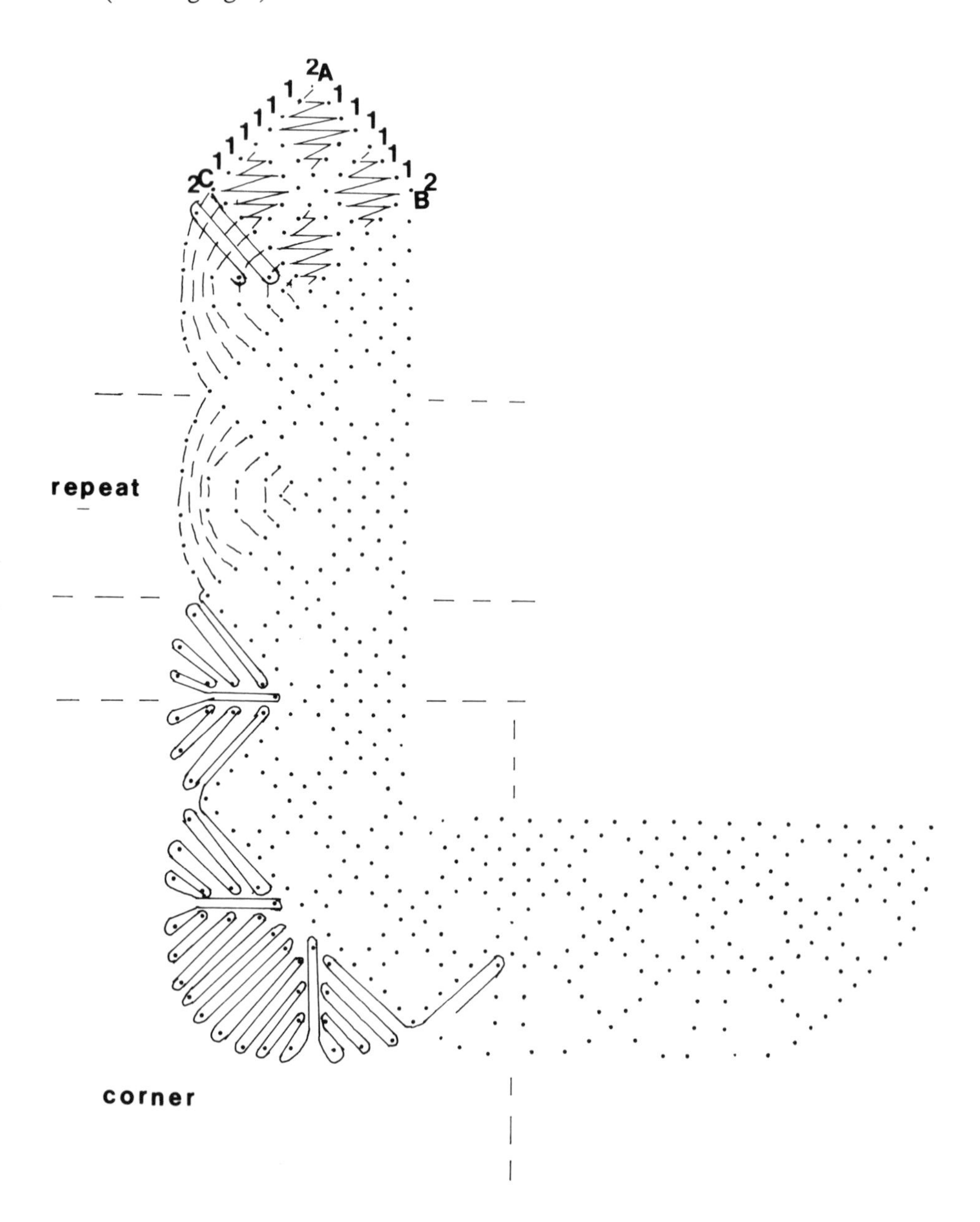

Rose

Madiera Tanne 50

This may be used as a decoration on pockets, handkerchieves, skirts, dresses, etc.

Method of working

Trails

These are worked using seven pairs, with cloth stitch and twist footsides. Start as in *PS*, Section I, 6. Work in the order A to E.

Leaves F and G

1. Hang on six pairs and increase to eleven or twelve pairs.
2. For start and footsides see *PS*, Sections I, 5 and I, 37.

Fillings

Use Torchon ground, as in *BBLS*, page 12.

Flower centre

This uses single twisted pairs which cross in cloth stitch and twist.

NB: The larger pricking was worked, so for the small size reduce the number of pairs accordingly. Thicker threads may be used for the larger size, in which case also reduce the number of pairs to adjust density.

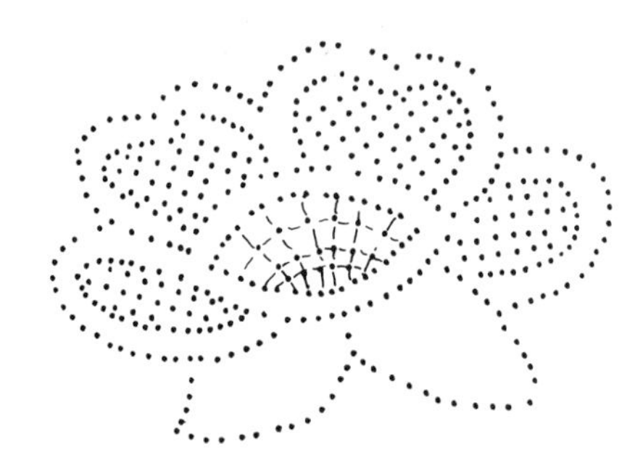

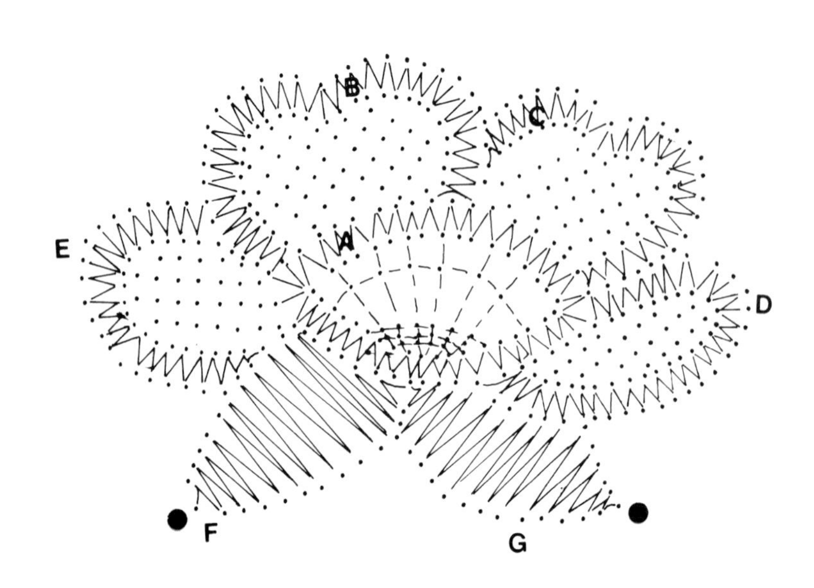

Bowl of tulips

Bockens 90

A picture for framing.

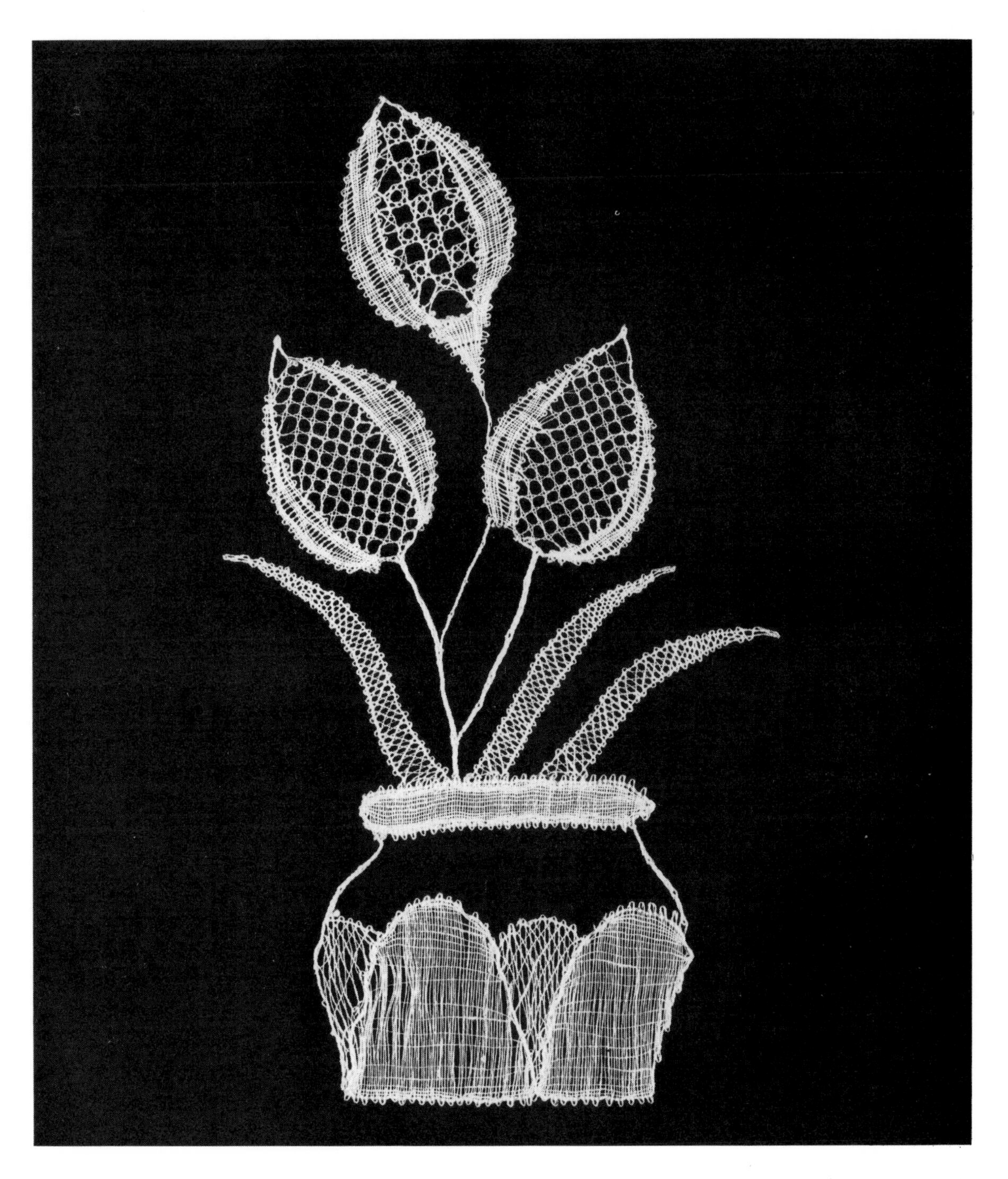

Method of working

Vase

1. Rim: hang on five pairs, increase to nine pairs and work in cloth stitch.
2. Base:
   i) Hang on three pairs, work in cloth stitch or half stitch increasing to keep the density even. This may be as thin or thick as required.
   ii) Work footsides in cloth stitch and twist.
   iii) Decrease as necessary, leaving these pairs off to be worked in the next section. Work as in (i) to complete the base.
3. Work half stitch plaits to join the base and rim.

Leaves

Hang on three pairs, increase to seven pairs and work in half stitch.

Flowers

1. Hang on four pairs open and work half stitch plaits to right and left. Add six pairs as necessary and work the petals in cloth stitch.
2. A textured effect is obtained by adding twists to the weavers.
3. The centres may be worked in rose ground 4 or Torchon ground (*BBLS*, pages 68, 12) or variations of these.
4. The base of the central flower (calyx) is worked with pairs from the outer petals, reducing to two pairs for the stalks worked as half stitch plaits.
5. –/–/–/ shows half stitch plaits on the pattern.

NB: This design can also be worked effectively in coloured threads.

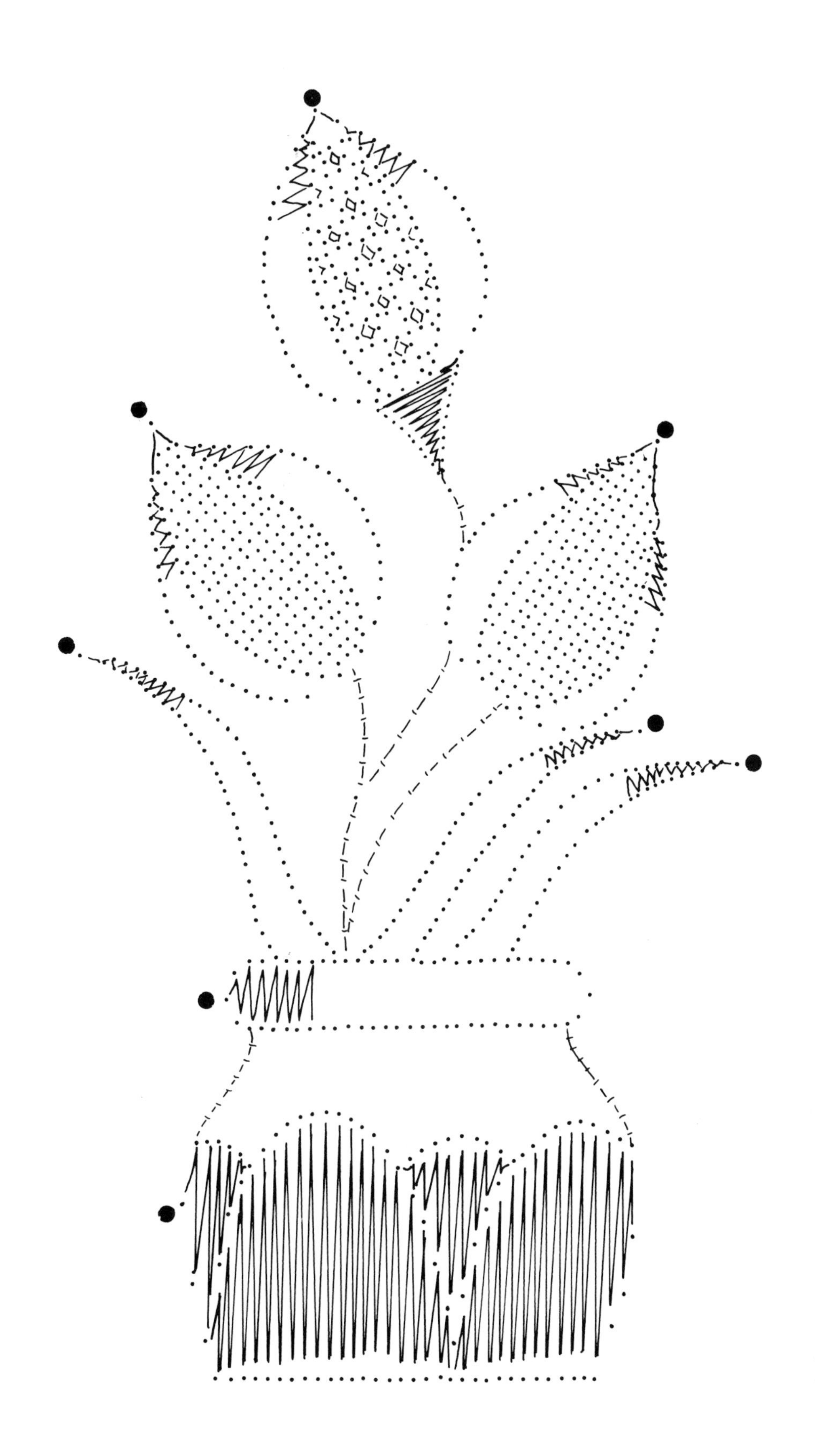

Bridge coasters

Madiera Tanne 30

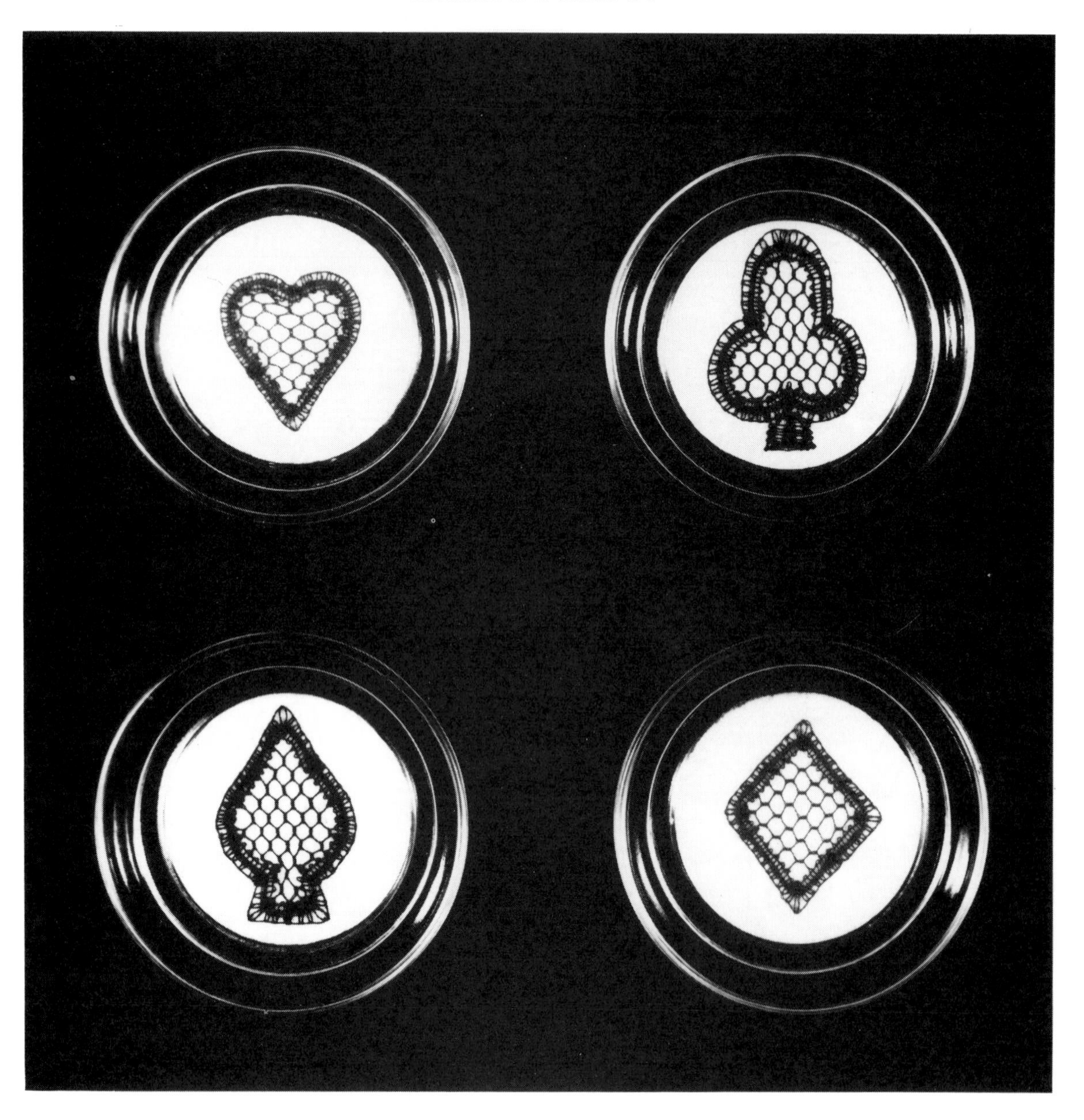

Method of working

Braids

1. Hang on five pairs. See *PS*, Sections I, 6 and I, 37 for start and outer footside, doing cloth stitch and twist on the inner footside.
2. Where a pin has to be used more than once, see *PS*, Section VII, 18.

Fillings

Use Torchon double ground – *BBLS*, page 23.

'Club' stalk

Use 10 pairs and work in cloth stitch, decreasing as necessary.

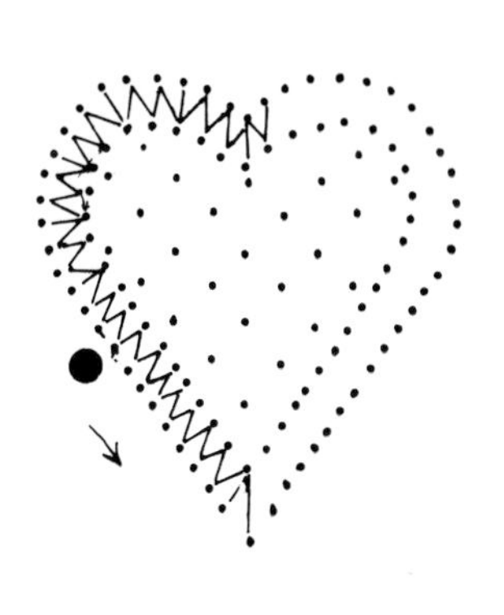

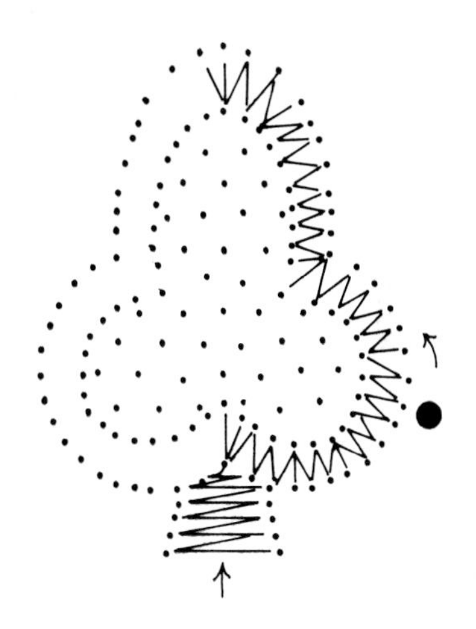

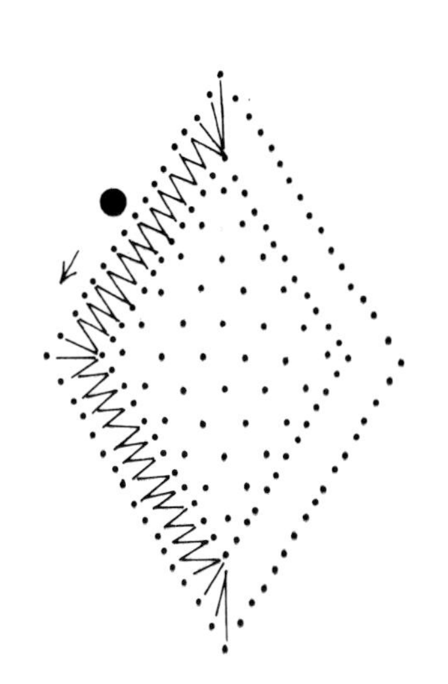

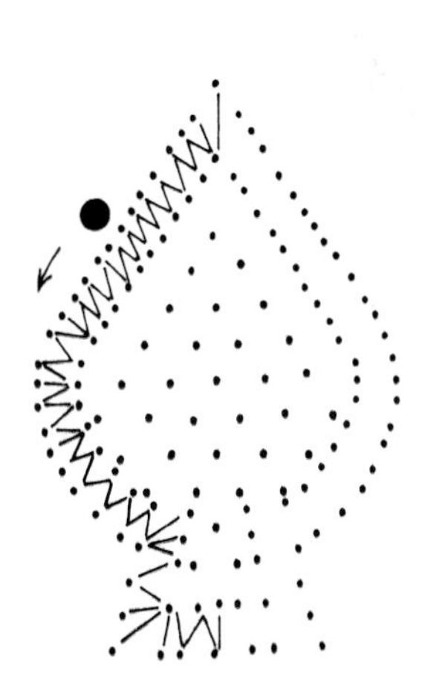

Corner motif 1

Brok 80

This may be used as a handkerchief corner, or as a decoration on a handbag, pocket or the front of a dress. Worked in a stiffer thread and mounted, it can also be made up into a bridal head-dress.

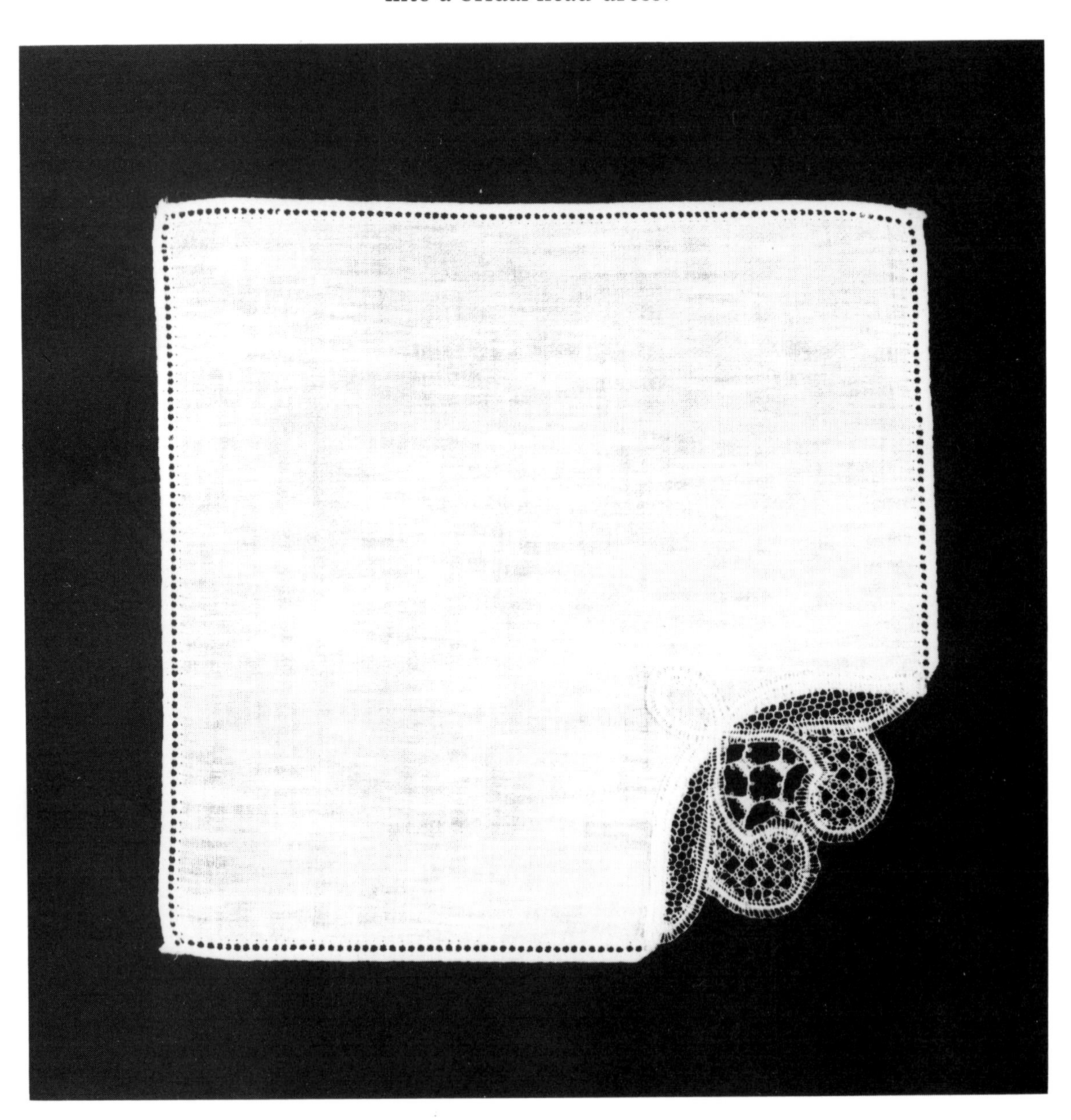

Method of working

Trail A

1. Using five pairs, hang on as in *PS*, Sections I, 6 and I, 37, with a cloth stitch and twist inner footside.
2. Where the trails cross, follow *PS*, Section IV, 82a.
3. Work to the last twelve pins. Put these pairs to one side.

Trails B and C

1. Work as for trail A.
2. When trail B has been worked, trail A may be finished, bowing off neatly into trail B.

Fillings

1. For trails B and C, use point ground.
2. For D, use rose ground 4 (*BBLS*, page 68).
3. Centre, use brick and picot (*BBLS*, page 144).

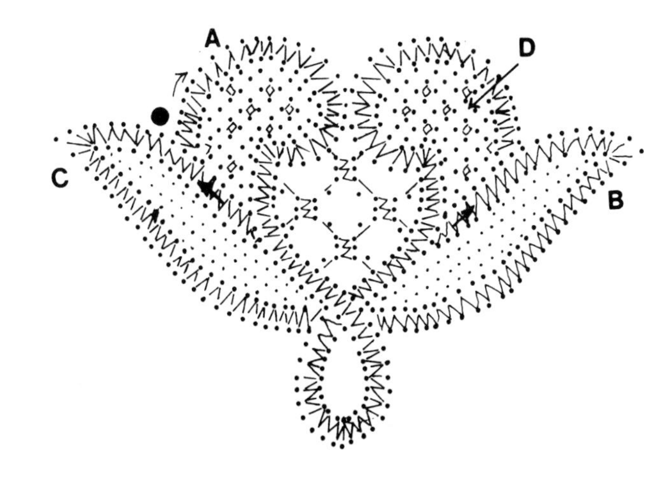

Corner motif 2

BOUC Fil à dentelle 100

Uses are the same as for Corner motif 1.

Method of working

1. Work the trails, using five pairs, in the order 1 to 5, with cloth stitch and twist footsides.
2. The filling used is point ground. If alternative fillings are used, these can be pricked on transparent film, and then put on to the pricking for use.

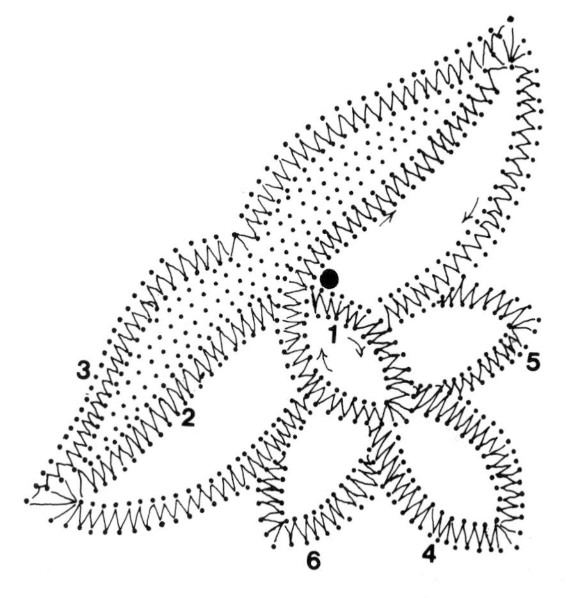

Motif 3

DMC Fil à dentelle 80

This may be used to decorate handbags, pockets, etc, and can have an initial inserted in the centre.

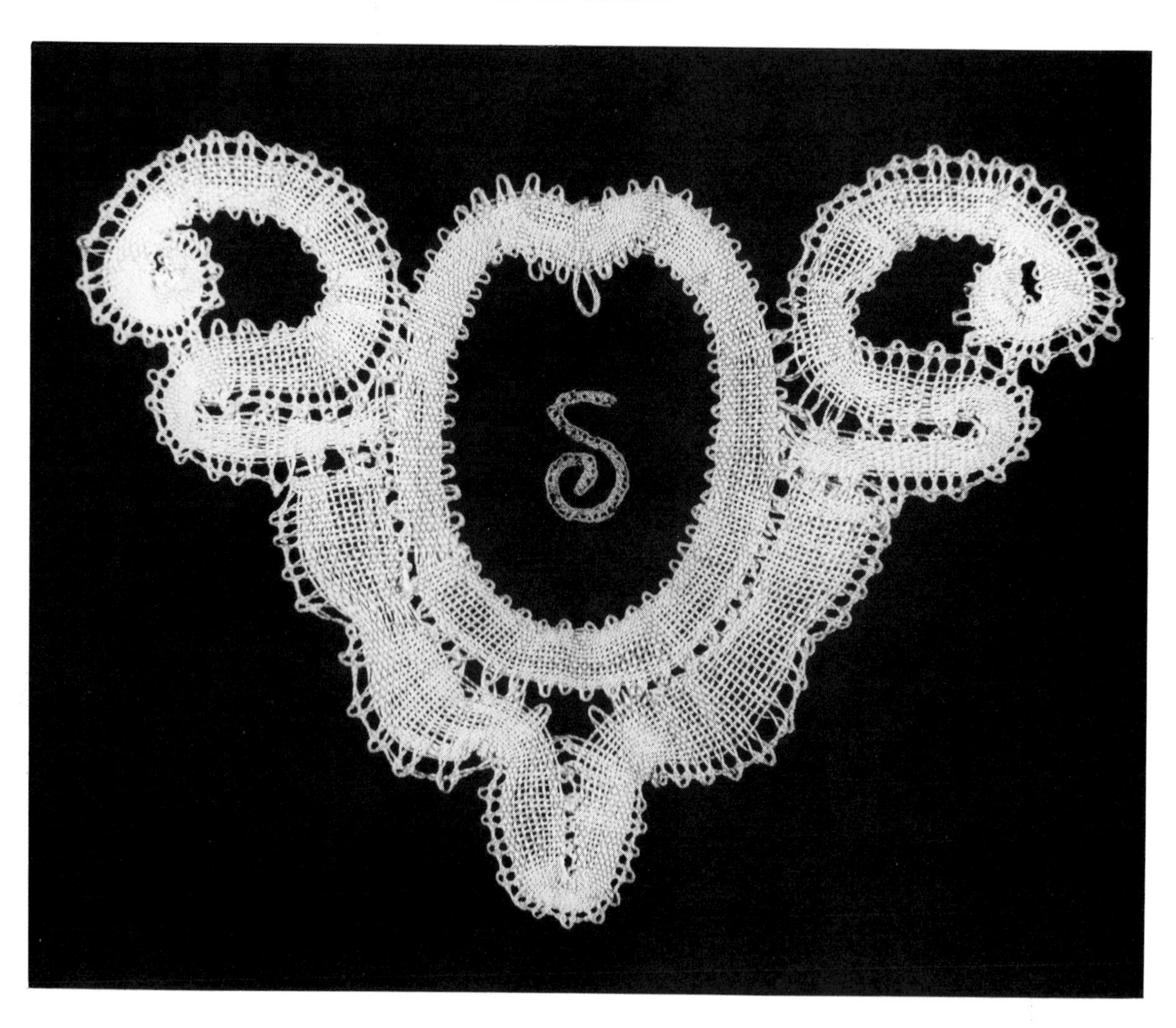

Method of working

Trail A

Hang on eight pairs as in *PS*, Sections I, 6 and I, 37. Work in cloth stitch.

Trail B

Start as *PS* Section I, 34 and use eight pairs.

Trail C

Hang on eight pairs and work as other trails.

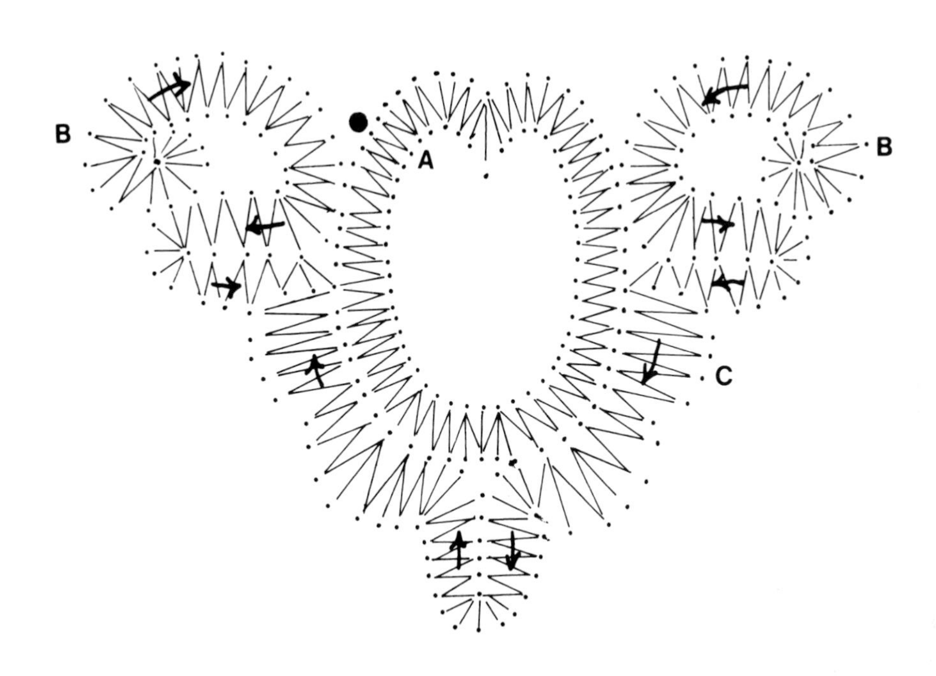

Decoration

Bockens 80/2

This may be used to enhance skirts, jackets, blouse pockets, bags, etc.

Method of working

1. The trails are worked in the order A to F.
2. Use five pairs for the trails. These may be worked in either half stitch, cloth stitch or a combination of both.
3. Half stitch plaits and picots join trails B and C.
4. The central motif may also be used separately.

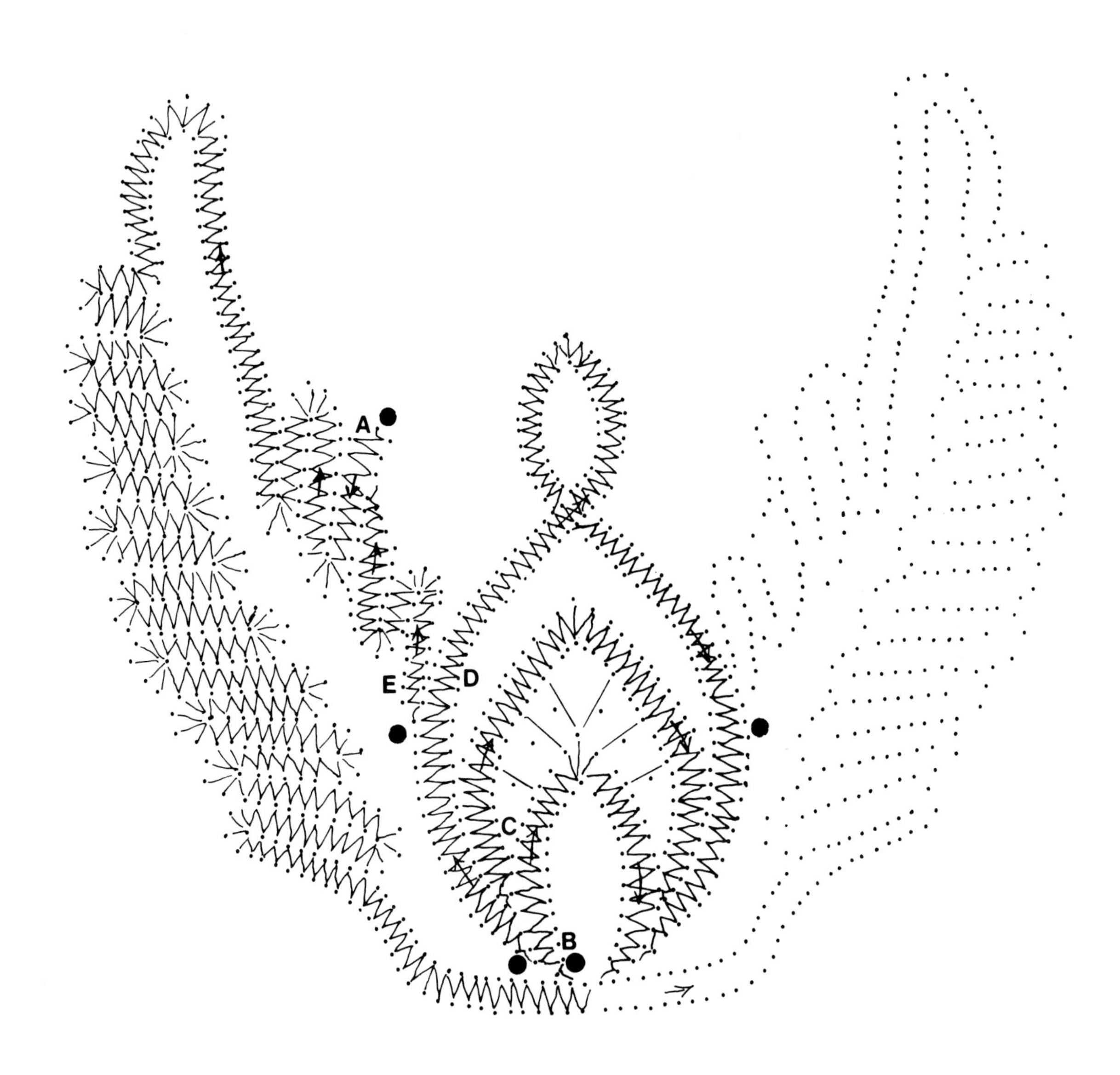

Table mat 1

Bockens 60/2

This has been designed so that it may be used as one complete design, or parts used separately for differing uses. A and G may be used for pendants; B would be ideal for coasters; the whole centre, bounded by scrolls C, can be used as small mats; the complete motif can also be repeated and joined together – or alternated with linen squares – to make a larger piece.

Method of working

Centre motif A

1. Lay twelve pairs laterally on the pillow slightly above pin N. With the centre two pairs work a half stitch plait and picots to the middle.
2. With the right-hand four pairs work a half stitch plait and picots to the right as two individual plaits.
3. Repeat for the left-hand pairs.
4. Add two pairs at P, Q and R. Work these in half stitch plaits and picots to the centre.
5. Work the centre in half stitch.
6. Work half stitch plaits and picots from the centre to meet the outer plaits and bow off as necessary.
7. Use the plaits from Motif A to work the next circle of half stitch plaits and picots that form the outer edge of Motif B.

Scroll C

1. Hang on two pairs, work a half stitch plait and then add three extra pairs for the scroll which is worked in cloth stitch.
2. Bow in to support pin for initial half stitch plait.
3. Reduce to two pairs, work half stitch plait and bow off into the scroll.

Circle D

1. Using five pairs, work in cloth stitch, with cloth stitch and twist footsides. Start as in *PS*, Section I, 6.
2. Bow into Scroll C where these touch.

Scroll E

1. Hang on six pairs, work as for the Scroll in *BFL*, page 87.
2. Bow into Scroll C where necessary.
3. Two of these scrolls have been worked in a finer thread (Bockens 90) to show the difference this makes.

Circle F

Use five pairs, work in half stitch. Start as for Circle D.

Circle G

1. Start as for Circle D, using five pairs. The outer footside is worked in cloth stitch and twist, the inner as *PS*, Section I, 37.
2. As in the central motif, pairs are hung on as the outer trail is worked. After the centre has been worked, these pairs are taken back into the outer trail and then left off.
3. Sew into Scrolls C and E as necessary.

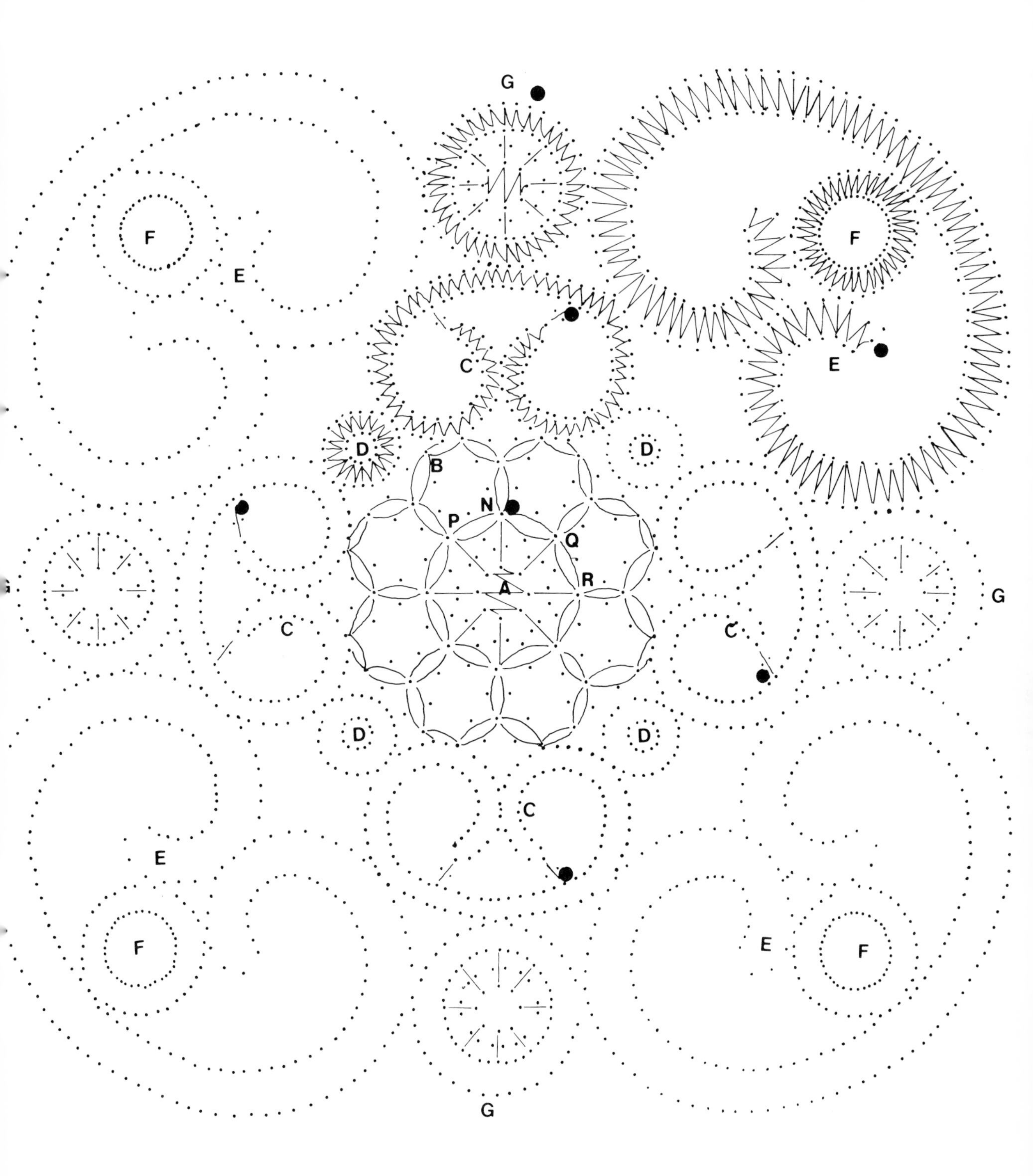
G
F
E
F
C
E
D
D
B
N
P
Q
G
A
R
G
C
C
D
D
C
E
F
E
F
G

Poppy

Bockens 90

This may be worked as a picture, or by joining two pieces end to end to make a large mat.

Method of working

Order of working: Trail A, Trail B, Leaves C and D, Flower J, Leaves E, F and G, Leaves H and I.

Trail A

Hang on six pairs and work as in *PS*, Section I, 6 using cloth stitch.

Trail B

Hang on six pairs, work in cloth stitch with footsides as in *PS*, Section I, 37.

Leaves C and G

1. Hang on four pairs and increase to nine pairs (see *PS*, Section I, 16) Work in half stitch.
2 Bow off into Trail B.

Leaves D and F

Hang on four pairs and start as in *PS*, Section I, 16. Increase to fifteen pairs using footsides as in Trail B.

Flower J

Work as in *BFL*, page 64, using five pairs for the centre trail and twelve pairs for the petals.

Leaf E

1. Bow two pairs into Flower J, work a half stitch plait and picot.
2. Use the pairs from this plait to start the leaf, increasing to twelve pairs and working in half stitch.

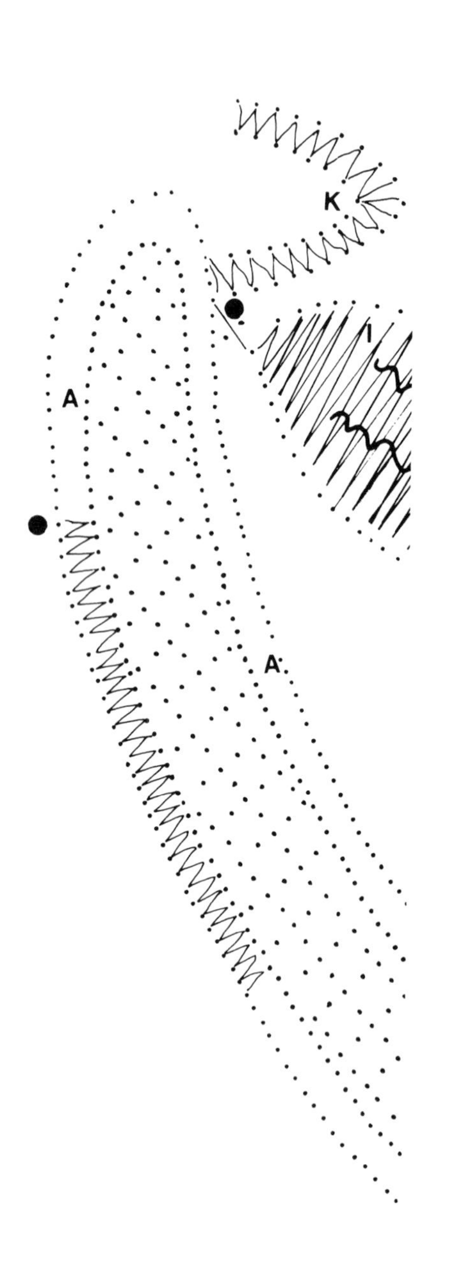

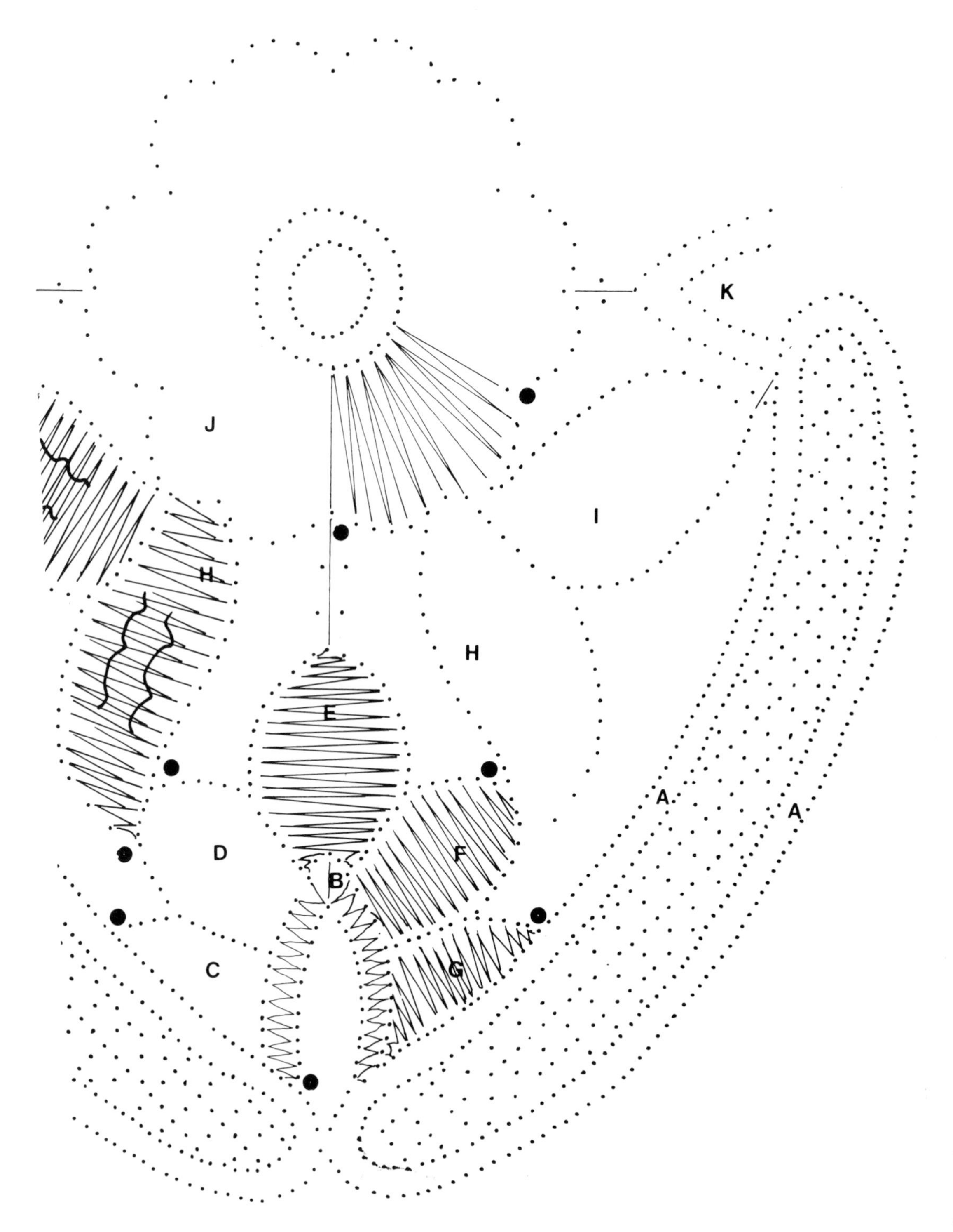
K
J
I
H
H
E
A
A
D
F
B
C
G

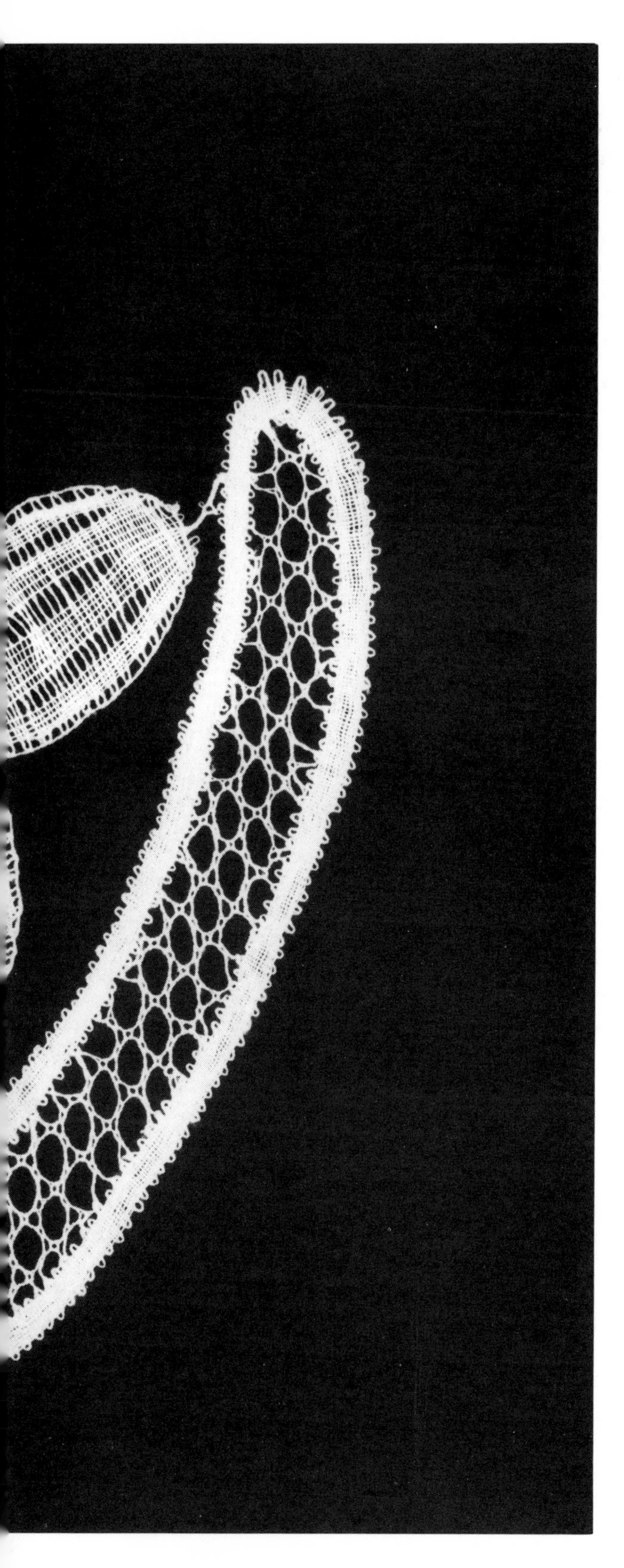

Leaves H and I

Work these using fourteen pairs and footsides as in Trail B. Twists on the weavers may be used to give texture to the leaf. A half stitch plait is used to start Leaf I as for Leaf E.

Trail K

1. Hang on six pairs and work with cloth stitch and twist footsides.
2. Join to Flower J with half stitch plait and picots.
3. This trail is only needed if a mat is being worked, and links the Trails A in the two halves.

Sunburst

Madiera Tanne 30

A picture for framing.

Method of working

1. Commence with the upper scrolls (three or four pairs, depending on size). Work in cloth stitch with half stitch plaits for the stalks treating each pair as a single bobbin.
2. Use the pairs from the upper scrolls to work the centre 'sun' in half stitch, bowing out those not required.
3. Where the stalks cross each other, work a four-plait crossing.
4. The lower scrolls are worked with pairs coming out of the centre, extra pairs being added as necessary.
5. The fine tendrils are single twisted pairs (–/–/–/ on the pattern).

Oval mat

Bockens 90

This can be a white mat, or can be worked in colours to enhance the floral motif.

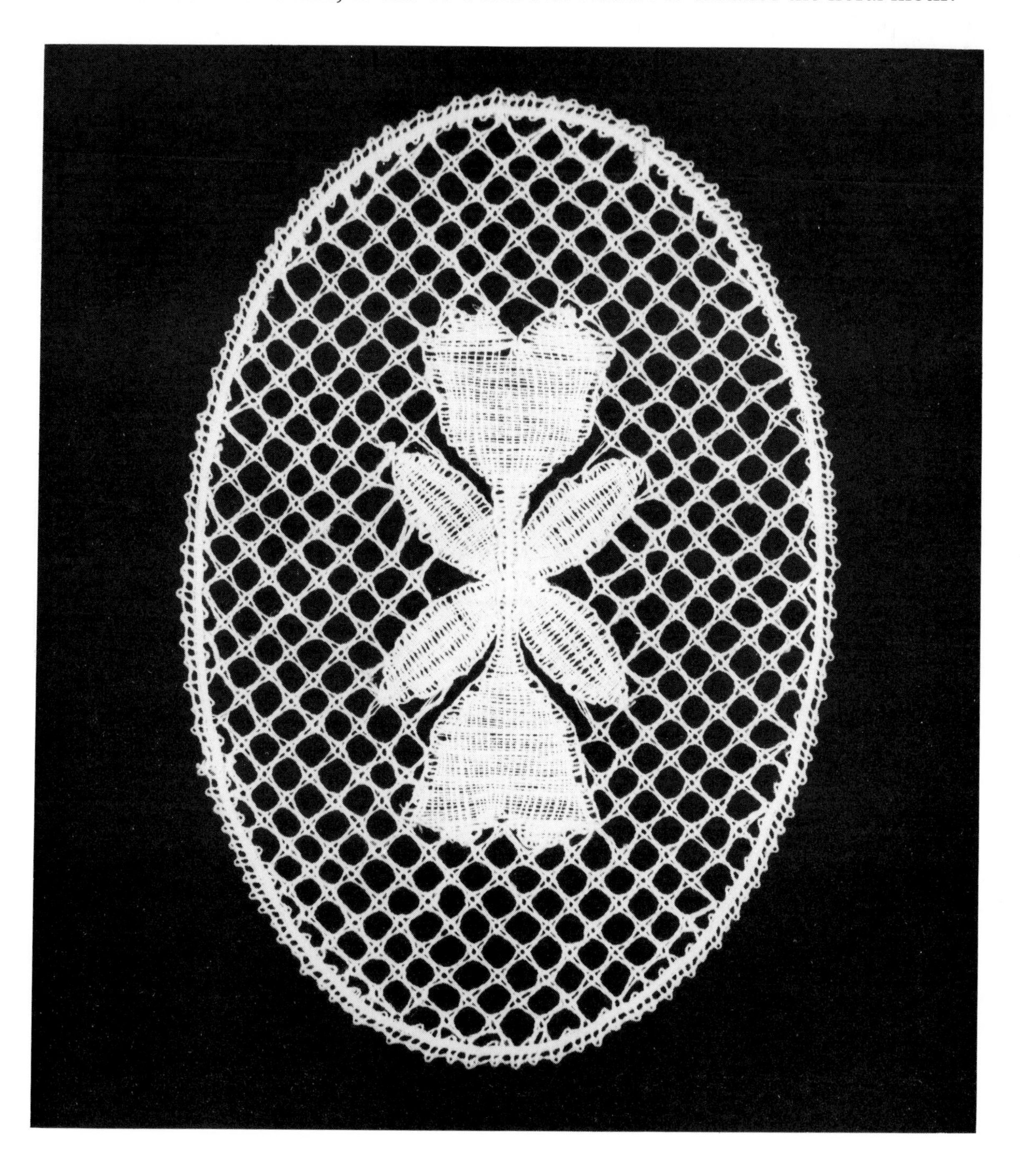

Method of working

Outer braid

1. Hang on four pairs as in *PS*, Section I, 6.
2. Work in cloth stitch with cloth stitch and twist on the outer footside.

Centre flower

1. Hang on four pairs at each apex as in *PS*, Section I, 16, and increase to fifteen pairs.
2. At '**A**' the weavers meet; one will become a passive and the other will continue to work as the weaver.
3. Reduce to five pairs for the stalk and then increase to fifteen pairs for the second flower.
4. Work the reverse of (2) at the base of the flower.

Leaves

1. Hang on four pairs as in Centre Flower (1) and increase to eight pairs.
2. Work in cloth stitch adding twists to weavers for texturing.

Ground

1. Use cane ground as in *BBLS*, page 29.

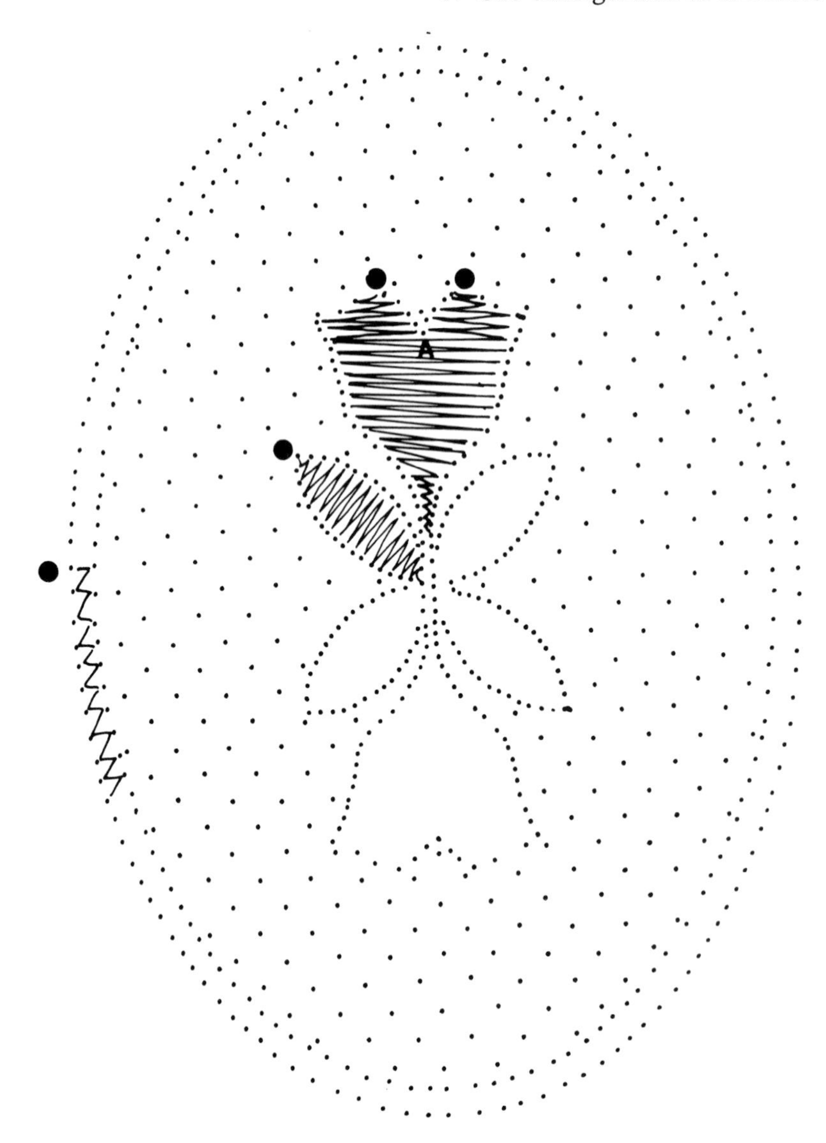

Fan

The outer trail and the ground were worked in DMC fil à dentelle for greater strength. The flowers and leaves are worked in Madiera tanne 50. By joining and overlapping two complete prickings a circle may be made. This can then be used to make a large mat which can have a linen centre or this can be provided by the table mat on page 84. A 1 cm separation has been allowed and the two pieces may be joined by the use of faggotting, etc.

Method of working

Outer trail

1. Hang on seven pairs as in *PS* Section I, 6.
2. Work in cloth stitch with cloth stitch and twist footsides.

Flowers

1. Use *BFL* techniques, pages 63 and 66.
2. The number of pairs required will depend on the thickness of thread used.

Stalks

1. Work as for *BFL* page 87, using five pairs.
2. Reduce to five pairs where the stalks join.
3. Work in cloth stitch.

Leaves

1. Work the outer pair as *BFL*, page 86.
2. Use eight pairs and work in cloth stitch.
3. Work the inner leaf as *BFL*, page 79.
4. Using five pairs, work in half stitch.

Ground

Use Dieppe Ground *BBLS*, page 12.

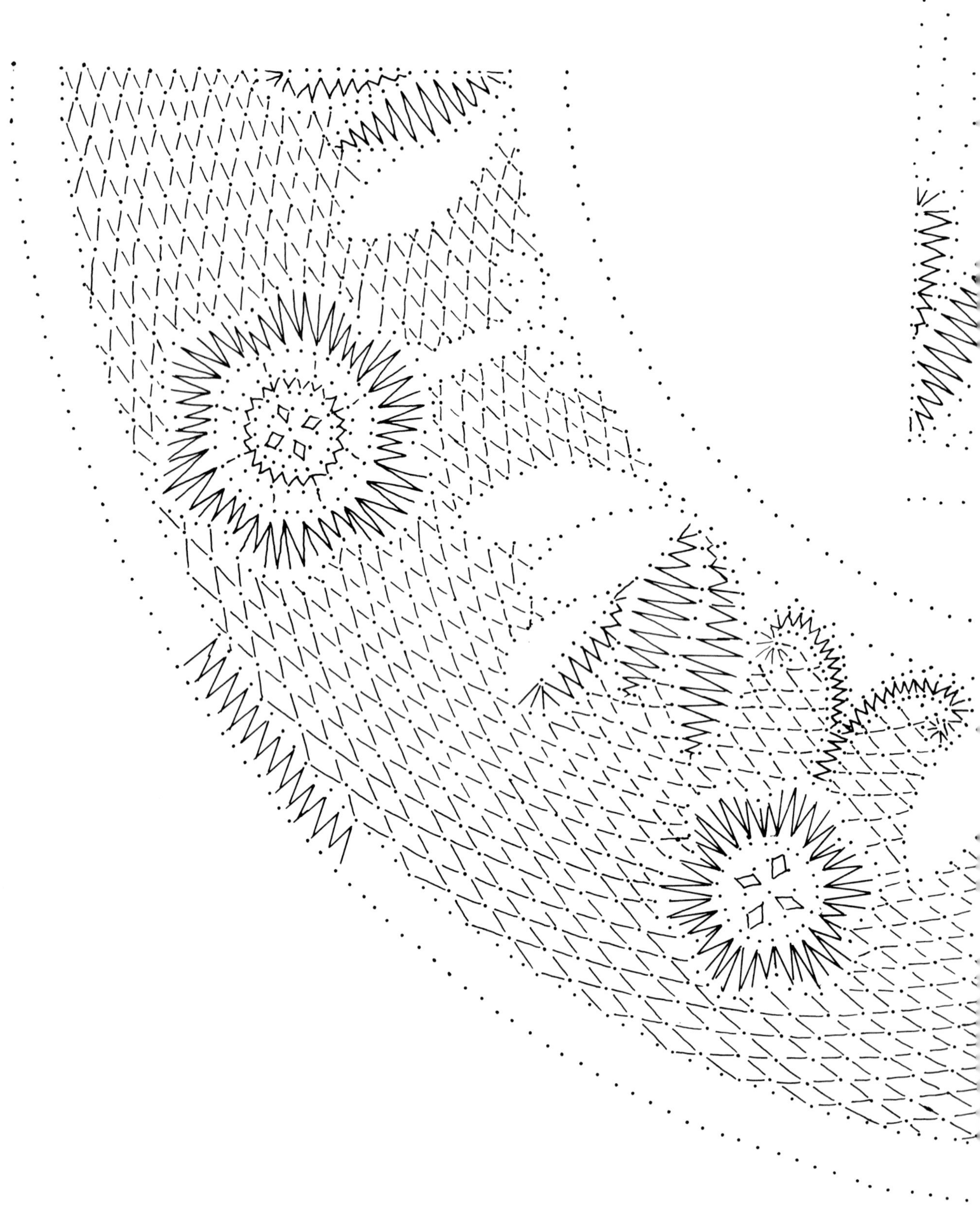

Table mat 2

Campbells 70

This may be used by itself as a table mat, or as the centre of the large mat formed by joining two fan patterns, as on page 79, in which case use either cotton throughout or linen throughout. The centre motif may also be used as a pendant. This can also be enhanced by using coloured thread.

Method of working

Outer trail

Hang on eight pairs and work as *PS*, Section I, 6 with cloth stitch and twist footsides.

Central motif

1. Hang on five pairs, work as for the outer trail with inner footside in cloth stitch.
2. At the same time, hang on twelve pairs to work half stitch plaits and picots for the centre half stitch circle.
3. Finish the centre trail bringing in the plaits and then leaving off pairs to keep the total to five.

Flowers

Use seven pairs and work as in *BFL* (Flower no. 2, page 63).

Stalks

1. Use four pairs and work as scroll in *BFL*, page 87.
2. Where the scrolls join, reduce to six pairs.
3. Work in cloth stitch.

Leaves

1. Work the outer pair as in *BFL*, page 86, using eight pairs. Work in cloth stitch.
2. Work the inner leaf as in *BFL*, page 79, in half stitch using five pairs.

Ground

1. Use Dieppe Ground, *BBLS*, page 12 until the pins crowd. Then change to Torchon ground.

Suppliers and sources of information

General Suppliers:

United Kingdom

Alby Lace Museum
Cromer Road
Alby
Norfolk
NR11 7QE

Busy Bobbins
Unit 7
Scarrots Lane
Newport
Isle of Wight
PO30 1JD

Chosen Crafts Centre
46 Winchcombe Street
Cheltenham
Gloucestershire
GL52 2ND

Jo Firth
Lace Marketing & Needlecraft Supplies
58 Kent Crescent
Lowtown
Pudsey
West Yorkshire
LS28 9EB

J. & J. Ford
October Hill
Upper Way
Upper Longdon
Rugeley
Staffordshire
WS15 1QB

Framecraft
83 Hampstead Road
Handsworth Wood
Birmingham
B2 1JA

Doreen Gill
14 Barnfield Road
Petersfield
Hampshire
GU31 4DQ

R. Gravestock
Highwood
Crews Hill
Alfrick
Worcestershire
WR6 5HF

The Handicraft Shop
47 Northgate
Canterbury
Kent
CT1 1BE

Frank Herring & Sons
27 High West Street
Dorchester
Dorset
DT1 1UP

Honiton Lace Shop
44 High Street
Honiton
Devon

D. J. Hornsby
149 High Street
Burton Latimer
Kettering
Northamptonshire
NN15 5RL

also at:
25 Manwood Avenue
Canterbury
Kent
CT2 7AH

Frances Iles
73 High Street
Rochester
Kent
ME1 1LX

Jane's Pincushions
Unit 4
Taverham Crafts
Taverham Nursery Centre
Fir Covent Road
Taverham
Norwich
NR8 6HT

Loricraft
19 Peregrine Way
Grove
Wantage
Oxfordshire

Needlestyle
5 The Woolmead
Farnham
Surrey
GU9 7TX

Needlestyle
24–26 West Street
Alresford
Hampshire

Needlework
Ann Bartlett
Bucklers Farm
Coggeshall
Essex
CO6 1SB

Needle and Thread
80 High Street
Horsell
Woking
Surrey
GU21 4SZ

The Needlewoman
21 Needles Alley
off New Street
Birmingham
B2 5AE

T. Parker
124 Corhampton Road
Boscombe East
Bournemouth
Dorset
BH6 5NZ

Jane Playford
North Lodge
Church Close
West Runton
Norfolk
NR27 9QY

Redburn Crafts
Squires Garden Centre
Halliford Road
Upper Halliford
Shepperton
Middlesex
TW17 8RU

Christine Riley
53 Barclay Street
Stonehaven
Kincardineshire
Scotland

Peter & Beverley Scarlett
Strupak
Hill Head
Cold Wells
Ellon
Grampian
Scotland

Ken & Pat Schultz
134 Wisbech Road
Thornley
Peterborough

J. S. Sear
Lacecraft supplies
8 Hill View
Sherrington
Buckinghamshire
MK16 9NY

Sebalace
Waterloo Mills
Howden Road
Silsden
West Yorkshire
BD2 ONA

A. Sells
49 Pedley Lane
Clifton
Shefford
Bedfordshire

Shireburn Lace
Finkle Court
Finkle Hill
Sherburn in Elmet
North Yorkshire
LS25 6EB

SMP
4 Garners Close
Chalfont St Peter
Buckinghamshire
SL9 OHB

Southern Handicrafts
20 Kensington Gardens
Brighton
Sussex
BN1 4AC

Spangles
Carole Morris
Burwell
Cambridgeshire
CB5 OED

Stitches
Dovehouse Shopping Parade
Warwick Road
Olton
Solihull
West Midlands

Teazle Embroideries
35 Boothferry Road
Hull
North Humberside

Valley House Crafts Studios
Ruston
Scarborough
North Yorkshire

George Walker
The Corner Shop
Rickinghall
Diss
Norfolk

West End Lace Supplies
Ravensworth Court Road
Mortimer West End
Reading
Berkshire
RG7 3UD

George White Lacemakers' Supplies
40 Heath Drive
Boston Spa
West Yorkshire
L23 6PB

Bobbins

A. R. Arches
The Poplars
Shetland
near Stowmarket
Suffolk
IP14 3DE

T. Brown
Temple Lane Cottage
Littledean
Cinderford
Gloucestershire

Chrisken Bobbins
26 Cedar Drive
Kingsclere
Buckinghamshire
RG15 8TD

Malcolm J. Fielding
2 Northern Terrace
Moss Lane
Silverdale
Lancashire
LA5 OST

Richard Gravestock
Highwood
Crews Hill
Alfrick
Worcestershire
WR6 5HF

Larkfield Crafts
Hilary Rickitts
4 Island Cottages
Mapledurwell
Basingstoke
Hampshire
RG25 2LU

Loricraft
19 Peregrine Way
Grove
Wantage
Oxfordshire

T. Parker
124 Corhampton Road
Boscombe East
Bournemouth
Dorset
BH6 5NZ

Bryan Phillips
Pantglas
Cellan
Lampeter
Dyfed
SA48 8JD

D. H. Shaw
47 Lamor Crescent
Thrushcroft
Rotherham
South Yorkshire
S66 9QD

Sizelands
1 Highfield Road
Winslow
Buckinghamshire
MK10 3QU

Christine & David Springett
21 Hillmorton Road
Rugby
Warwickshire
CV22 5DF

Richard Viney
Unit 7
Port Royal Street
Southsea
Hampshire
PO5 3UD

West End Lace Suppliers
Ravensworth Court Road
Mortimer West End
Reading
Berkshire
RG7 3UD

Lace Pillows

Newnham Lace Equipment
15 Marlowe Close
Basingstoke
Hampshire
RG24 9DD

Books

Christopher Williams
19 Morrison Avenue
Parkstone
Poole
Dorset
BH17 4AD

Silk embroidery and lace thread

E. & J. Piper
Silverlea
Flax Lane
Glemsford
Suffolk
CO10 7RS

Silk weaving yarn

Hilary Chetwynd
Kipping Cottage
Cheriton
Alresford
Hampshire
SO24 OPW

Frames and mounts

Doreen Campbell
Highcliff
Brenisham Road
Malmesbury
Wiltshire

Matt coloured transparent adhesive film

Heffers Graphic Shop
26 King Street
Cambridge
CB1 1LN

Linen by the metre (yard) and made up articles of church linen

Mary Collins
Church Furnishings
St Andrews Hall
Humber Doucy Lane
Ipswich
Suffolk
IP4 3BP

Hayes & Finch
Head Office & Factory
Hanson Road
Aintree
Liverpool
L9 9BP

United States of America

Arbor House
22 Arbor Lane
Roslyn Hights
NY 11577

Baltazor Inc.
3262 Severn Avenue
Metairie
LA 7002

Beggars' Lace
P.O. Box 17263
Denver
Colorado 80217

Berga Ullman Inc.
P.O. Box 918
North Adams
Massachusetts 01247

Frederick J. Fawcett
129 South Street
Boston
Massachusetts 02130

Frivolité
15526 Densmore N.
Seattle
Washington 98113

Happy Hands
3007 S. W. Marshall
Pendleton
Oregon 97180

International Old Lacers
P.O. Box 1029
Westminster
Colorado 80030

Lace Place de Belgique
800 S. W. 17th Street
Boca Raton
FL 33432

Lacis
2150 Stuart Street
Berkeley
California 9470

Robin's Bobbins
RTL Box 1736
Mineral Bluff
Georgia 30559

Robin and Russ
Handweavers
533 North Adams Street
McMinnvills
Oregon 97128

Some Place
2990 Adline Street
Berkeley
California 94703

Osma G. Todd Studio
319 Mendoza Avenue
Coral Gables
Florida 33134

The Unique And Art Lace Cleaners
5926 Delman Boulevard
St Louis
Missouri 63112

Van Scriver Bobbin Lace
130 Cascadilla Park
Ithaca
New York 14850

The World in Stitches
82 South Street
Milford
NH 03055

Australia

Dentelles Lace Supplies
3 Narrak Close
Jindalee
Queensland 4074

The Lacemaker
94 Fordham Avenue
Hartwell
Victoria 3124

Spindle and Loom
Arcade 83
Longueville Road
Lane Cove
NSW 2066

Tulis Crafts
201 Avoca Street
Randwick
NSW 2031

Belgium

't Handwekhuisje
Katelijnestraat 23
8000 Bruges

Kantcentrum
Balstraat 14
8000 Bruges

Manufacture Belge de Dentelle
6 Galerie de la Reine
Galeries Royales St Hubert
1000 Bruxelles

Orchidée
Mariastraat 18
8000 Bruges

Ann Thys
't Apostelientje
Balstraat 11
8000 Bruges

France

Centre d'Initiations à la Dentelle du Puy
2 Rue Duguesclin
43000 Le Puy en Velay

A L'Econome
Anne-Marie Deydier
Ecole de Dentelle aux Fuseaux
10 rue Paul Chenavard
69001 Lyon

Rougier and Plé
13–15 bd des Filles de Calvaire
75003 Paris

West Germany

Der Fenster Laden
Berliner Str. 8
D 6483 Bad Soden
Salmunster

P. P. Hempel
Ortolanweg 34
1000 Berlin 47

Heikona De Ruijter
Kleoppelgrosshandel
Langer Steinweg 38
D4933 Blomberg

Holland

Blokker's Boektiek
Bronsteeweg 4/4a
2101 AC Heemstede

Theo Brejaat
Postbus 5199
3008 AD Rotterdam

Magazijn *De Vlijt*
Lijnmarkt 48
Utrecht

Switzerland

Fadehax
Inh. Irene Solca
4105 Biel-Benken
Basel

New Zealand

Peter McLeavey
P.O. Box 69.007
Auckland 8

Sources of Information

The Lace Guild
The Hollies
53 Audnam
Stourbridge
West Midlands
DY8 4AE

The Lace Society
Linwood
Stratford Road
Oversley
Alcester
Warwickshire
BY9 6PG

The British College of Lace
21 Hillmorton Road
Rugby
Warwickshire
CV22 5DF

The English Lace School
Oak House
Church Stile
Woodbury
Nr Exeter
Devon

International Old Lacers
President
Gunvor Jorgensen
366 Bradley Avenue
Northvale
NJ 076647
USA

United Kingdom Director of International Old Lacers
S. Hurst
4 Dollius Road
London
N3 1RG

Ring of Tatters
Mrs C. Appleton
Nonesuch
5 Ryeland Road
Ellerby
Saltburn by Sea
Cleveland
TS13 5LP

Books

The following are stockists of the complete Batsford/Dryad Press range:

Avon

Bridge Bookshop
7 Bridge Street
Bath
BA2 4AS

Waterstone & Co.
4–5 Milsom Street
Bath
BA1 1DA

Bedfordshire

Arthur Sells
Lane Cove
49 Pedley Lane
Clifton
Shefford
SG17 5QT

Berkshire

West End Lace Supplies
Ravensworth Court Road
Mortimer West End
Reading
RG7 3UD

Buckinghamshire

J. S. Sear Lacecraft Supplies
8 Hill View
Sherringham
MK16 9NY

Cambridgeshire

Dillons The Bookstore
Sydney Street
Cambridge

Cheshire

Lyn Turner
Church Meadow Crafts
15 Carisbrook Drive
Winsford
Cheshire

Devon

Creative Crafts & Needlework
18 High Street
Totnes
TQ9 5NP

Honiton Lace Shop
44 High Street
Honiton
EX14 8PJ

Dorset

F. Herring & Sons
High West Street
Dorchester
DT1 1UP

Tim Parker (mail order)
124 Corhampton Road
Boscombe East
Bournemouth
BH6 5NL

Durham

Lacemaid
6, 10 & 15 Stoneybeck
Bishop Middleham
County Durham
DL17 9BL

Gloucestershire

Southgate Handicrafts
68 Southgate Street
Gloucester
GL1 1TX

Waterstone & Co.
89–90 The Promenade
Cheltenham
GL50 1NB

Hampshire

Creative Crafts
11 The Square
Winchester
SO23 9ES

Doreen Gill
14 Barnfield Road
Petersfield
GU31 4DR

Larkfield Crafts
4 Island Cottages
Mapledurwell
Basingstoke
RG23 2LU

Needlestyle
24–26 West Street
Alresford

Ruskins
27 Bell Street
Romsey

Isle of Wight

Busy Bobbins
Unit 7
Scarrots Lane
Newport
PO30 1JD

Kent

The Handicraft Shop
47 Northgate
Canterbury

Frances Iles
73 High Street
Rochester
ME1 1LX

Lincolnshire

Rippingale Lace
Barn Farm House
Off Station Road
Rippingdale Bourne

London

Foyles
119 Charing Cross Road
WC2H OEB

Hatchards
187 Piccadilly
W1

Middlesex

Redburn Crafts
Squires Garden Centre
Halliford Road
Upper Halliford
Shepperton
TW17 8RU

Norfolk

Alby Lace Museum
Cromer Road
Alby
nr Aylsham
NR11 7QE

Jane's Pincushions
Taverham Craft Unit 4
Taverham Nursery Centre
Fir Covert Road
Taverham
Norwich
NR8 6HT

Waterstone & Co.
30 London Street
Norwich
NR2 1LD

Northamptonshire

D. J. Hornsby
149 High Street
Burton Latimer
Kettering
NN15 5RL

Oxfordshire

Loricraft
19 Peregrine Way
Grove
Wantage

Scotland

Embroidery Shop
51 Withain Street
Edinburgh
Lothian
EH3 7LW

Beverley Scarlett
Strupak
Hillhead
Coldwells
Ellon
Aberdeenshire

Waterstone & Co.
236 Union Street
Aberdeen
AB1 1TN

Surrey

Needlestyle
5 The Woolmead
Farnham
GU9 1TN

Sussex

Southern Handicrafts
20 Kensington Gardens
Brighton
BN1 4AL

Warwickshire

Christine & David Springett
21 Hillmorton Road
Rugby
CV22 6DF

North Yorkshire

Shireburn Lace
Finkel Court
Finkel Hill
Leeds
LS25 6EA

Valley House Craft Studios
Ruston
Scarborough

West Midlands

Needlewoman
21 Needles Alley
off New Street
Birmingham
B2 5AE

West Yorkshire

Sebalace
Waterloo Mill
Howden Road
Silsden
BD20 OHA

George White Lacemaking Supplies
40 Heath Drive
Boston Spa
LS23 6PB

Jo Firth
58 Kent Crescent
Lowtown
Pudsey
Leeds
LS28 9EB